SECRET DENVER

A Guide to the Weird, Wonderful, and Obscure

Eric Peterson and David Lewis

Reedy Press
PO Box 5131
St. Louis, MO 63139
www.reedypress.com

Library of Congress Control Number: 2020938249

ISBN: 9781681061054

Design by Jill Halpin

Printed in the United States of America
20 21 22 23 24 5 4 3 2 1

To Jamie,
Amphpath says he really, really likes you.
Love, Eric

To Marina with thanks, and to CTR, as ever.
David

CONTENTS

INTRODUCTION

At a mile above sea level, the thin air seems to catalyze the pace of peculiar happenings.

Or maybe it's the fact that Denver is the most isolated major city in the United States. You have to go more than 600 miles to get to a larger population center.

Whether it's the rarified air, the copious elbow room, or something else, the city has more than its fair share of secrets, puzzles, and oddities—and there are even more nestled on its outskirts on the plains and in the foothills of the Rockies.

The ever-evolving cityscape means some of Denver's secrets are ghosts of people and places that are no longer tangible. Other unusual attractions owe their existence to the local culture, cuisine, or economy.

Many of Denver's secrets are well kept. No one seems to know exactly what happened to a missing chunk of the largest gold nugget unearthed in Colorado or who robbed the Denver Mint in 1922. And the invention of the Denver omelet remains something of an open question.

From mysterious tunnels under the city to mountain peaks just outside of it, Denver has its share of secrets—and then some.

URBAN WILDERNESS

Where do buffalo roam at a former chemical weapons depot?

It's one thing for a city to have a sprawling wildlife refuge on its doorstep, and yet another for it to be a huge environmental success story as well.

Less than 10 miles northeast of downtown Denver, the place that is now the Rocky Mountain Arsenal National Wildlife Refuge was the site of a manufacturing facility for chemical weapons during World War II, leaving a seriously toxic legacy in its wake.

Starting in the early 1980s, the army and local and federal government agencies began a cleanup on the site that ultimately spanned three decades. After several bald eagle sightings, the US Fish and Wildlife Service designated it as an official national wildlife refuge in 1992.

When the cleanup was completed in 2010, the resulting 15,000-acre intersection of prairie, woodland, and wetland emerged as one of the largest urban wildlife refuges in the United States and a draw for wildlife watching and outdoor recreation. There's now a resident herd of bison, along with snapping turtles, deer, prairie dogs, black-footed ferrets, and nearly 300 species of birds.

Several popular fishing holes lure anglers, and the refuge also features more than 10 miles of hiking and walking trails. Many visitors take the 11-mile scenic drive that loops through

---

In 1961, crews drilled a well to a depth of 12,045 feet belowground to inject waste fluids, but the army discontinued the practice in 1966 because it triggered earthquakes.

Beginning in the 1940s, Rocky Mountain Arsenal served as a manufacturing facility for chemical weapons. Building 515 (pictured) served as a mustard gas facility. The entire site became the subject of a comprehensive cleanup project starting in the 1980s. Photo courtesy of Historic American Engineering Record, Library of Congress. https://www.loc.gov/resource/hhh.co0625.photos/?sp=3

Photo by Eric Peterson

bison pasture and delivers plenty of unobstructed views of the Rocky Mountains and downtown Denver. The visitor center is also worth a look, with exhibits on the refuge's history and ecology.

ROCKY MOUNTAIN ARSENAL NATIONAL WILDLIFE REFUGE

What: This urban wildlife haven is a huge environmental success story.

Where: 6550 Gateway Rd., Commerce City

Cost: Free

Pro Tip: Take the time to hike the 1.8-mile Ladora Loop Trail around Lake Ladora.

THE STRANGE CASE OF BUFFALO BILL'S BODY

Where is William "Buffalo Bill" Cody's final resting spot?

Western scout-turned-showman William "Buffalo Bill" Cody was the biggest celebrity of his day. Buffalo Bill's Wild West Show traveled the world in the late 1800s and early 1900s, presenting feats of horsemanship and marksmanship and all sorts of theatrics.

When Cody passed away in Denver in January 1917, his sister sold his body to the City of Denver and *The Denver Post* for $20,000. As the official story goes, Cody was finally put to rest when the ground thawed in June on Lookout Mountain outside Golden.

But according to the unofficial tall tale, three residents of Cody, Wyoming, the touristy town Buffalo Bill founded about 50 miles east of Yellowstone National Park, said the Colorado burial was not what Cody wanted. If you believe the story, they were able to secretly swap Cody's body for that of an anonymous cowboy. Rumor has it that the trio returned north to bury the real Cody on Cedar Mountain outside the town that bears his name.

Back on the official side of the story, a caravan later came down from Wyoming planning to take the body by force, but

---

You can visit Buffalo Bill's favorite bar in Denver, the Buckhorn Exchange (1000 Osage St.), as well as the spot where his body was kept on ice in 1917: the former Olinger Mortuary is now Linger Eatuary (2030 W. 30th Ave., see p. 124).

William "Buffalo Bill" Cody got his start as a scout for the railroad companies, but his legend soon grew, leading him into show business with his Wild West Show. At the time of his passing in 1917, he was one of the most recognizable people on Earth. Photo courtesy of Wikimedia Commons. https://commons.wikimedia.org/wiki/File:Cody-Buffalo-Bill-LOC.jpg

The gravesite of "Buffalo Bill" Cody near Golden, Colorado, is covered with 20 tons of concrete. It was seen as a deterrent to Wyomingites hell-bent on bringing his body back north to the town that bears his name. Photo courtesy of Carol Highsmith, Library of Congress. https://www.loc.gov/item/2011631818

officials in Colorado simply buried the grave under 20 tons of concrete, sealing its fate but shrouding it in mystery.

The debate continues today. Some say Cody is buried in Colorado, but there's a contingent who fiercely believe his real grave is located on Cedar Mountain.

BUFFALO BILL MUSEUM AND GRAVE

What: A museum illuminates the legendary Western showman's life at his alleged grave west of Denver.

Where: Lookout Mountain Park, 987 1/2 Lookout Mountain Rd., Golden

Cost: Adults, $5; seniors, $4; children ages 6–15, $1

Pro Tip: Explore Golden and its many attractions if you visit Lookout Mountain.

A LITERAL BOOMTOWN

Why didn't locals want to be by the railroad tracks at the wrong time?

The chemical conglomerate known as DuPont established Louviers (pronounced "loo-veers") as a company town south of Denver in 1906.

The name was taken from a DuPont company town in Delaware that was itself named for a member of the family's hometown in France (pronounced "loo-vee-ay"), but there wasn't just one moniker for Louviers. The DuPont factory, a.k.a. the Louviers Works, manufactured dynamite, nitroglycerin, and other explosives, earning the otherwise idyllic hamlet at the foot of the Rocky Mountains a menacing nickname: Hellsville. Locals for years worried that a truck full of nitroglycerin would stall out on the railroad tracks as a locomotive approached and result in a truly apocalyptic man-made eruption.

Business at the beginning was brisk, as the plant manufactured 300 tons of explosives a month in the early 20th century and 1,000 tons a month at its mid-century peak. There never was a cataclysmic truck-meets-train blast as feared, but explosions at the plant killed three workers in the early years of operation and seven more in the 1940s and 1970s.

The facility shut down once and for good in the 1980s, and the old taxidermy shop labeled "Hellsville, USA." is no longer, but there are still reminders of Louviers' fiery reputation in the

---

Between 1908 and 1971, the Louviers Works produced more than 1 billion pounds of dynamite. It was used by the US military as well as in mines in the Rockies.

A weathered wooden sign marking the entrance to the village of Louviers harks back to its legacy as a company town for DuPont and its factory for dynamite and other explosives. Photo courtesy of Jeffrey Beall, Creative Commons. https://en.wikipedia.org/wiki/File:Louviers,_Colorado.JPG

form of DuPont Park and the old Louviers Village Clubhouse, a remnant of the old company town that now houses a library and community center.

HELLSVILLE

What: The small town with an explosive nickname

Where: Twenty-six miles south of downtown Denver off of US Highway 85

Cost: Free

Pro Tip: Hit up Bud's Bar (54543 Manhart Ave. in nearby Sedalia) for a truly legendary cheeseburger.

BEYOND THE BIG TOP

What were the world's greatest showman's plans for the Denver neighborhood that still bears his name?

In 1878, Phineas T. Barnum, the circus tycoon and "World's Greatest Showman," bought 760 acres on the west side of Denver. He didn't spend much time in Colorado, but the self-proclaimed "Prince of Humbugs" was an avid investor who owned several other properties in the state at the time.

Rumors that Barnum wanted to winter his elephants on the land have lingered, but they're completely unfounded; his circus pachyderms spent their time off in lower, warmer places like Florida.

P. T. sold the land to his daughter, Helen Buchtel, who played a major role in developing a housing subdivision in what was at the time the independently incorporated city of Barnum, not Denver. Helen's husband, William Buchtel, served as mayor in the late 1880s.

However, Barnum was a bit slow to progress before it was connected with Denver by rail in 1893. The arrival of the trolley, followed by annexation by Denver three years later, spurred more development. A working-class community soon emerged.

The neighborhood's history came full circle in the 1990s when local activists pushed for a vacant lot to be transformed into a park. Artist Calvin Farrow created a sculpture of a

BARNUM IN DENVER

What: A neighborhood with a circus history

Where: Between 6th and Alameda Avenues and Federal Boulevard and Perry Street in west Denver

Cost: Free

Pro Tip: Check out the sun melting into the Rockies from Barnum Park. Denver's weekly *Westword* newspaper named it the "Best Place to Catch the Sunset" in 2019.

A working-class neighborhood on the west side of Denver, Barnum was never envisioned as a winter haven for P. T. Barnum's circus pachyderms; it was actually a bet on Denver real estate by the prolific investor. Photo courtesy of Jeffrey Beall, Creative Commons. https://commons.wikimedia.org/wiki/File:BarnumDenver.JPG

Superlative showman Phineas T. Barnum poses for a portrait with one of his biggest stars, General Tom Thumb, in 1850, more than a quarter-century before his real-estate exploits in Denver. Photo courtesy of Samuel Root or Marcus Aurelius Root, Wikimedia Commons. https://commons.wikimedia.org/wiki/File:Samuel_Root_or_Marcus_Aurelius_Root_-_P.T._Barnum_and_General_Tom_Thumb_-_Google_Art_Project-crop.jpg

joyous elephant ("Effie") and other circus-themed public art at the resulting Cedar Park (176 S. Knox Ct.). While real elephants never wintered in Denver, Effie is around for all four seasons.

While P. T. Barnum never spent much time in his namesake neighborhood, his legacy remains visible in the form of a circus-themed mural by street artist Pheud at the intersection of Lowell Boulevard and Alameda Avenue.

A DUBIOUS CULINARY LANDMARK

Was the cheeseburger really invented in Denver?

A number of other cities claim to be the site of the first cheeseburger ever flipped (Pasadena, California, and Louisville, Kentucky, are among them), but they don't have a snazzy granite marker like Denver's. (Pasadena does have a nice plaque, but it's no monument.)

Located at the former site of the barrel-shaped Humpty Dumpty drive-in, the first car-oriented eatery in the city, the monument tells the story of Louis Ballast serving the world's first cheeseburger. Make that "allegedly serving," as there's little evidence to back up the claim.

While naysayers are quick to point out the fact that many other chefs slapped a slice of cheese on a hunk of beef long before Ballast did, they didn't have the marketing mojo of the proprietor of the Humpty Dumpty. No matter where the cheeseburger was really born, Ballast was definitely the first alleged inventor to

THE CHEESEBURGER MONUMENT

What: A spot marking a dubious culinary claim

Where: 2776 Speer Blvd.

Cost: Free

Pro Tip: For a cheeseburger that would do Ballast proud, head to My Brother's Bar (2376 15th St.), the oldest continuously operating bar in Denver.

As the legend goes, Ballast first tried putting chocolate and peanut butter on his hamburgers before his "aha!" moment with cheese.

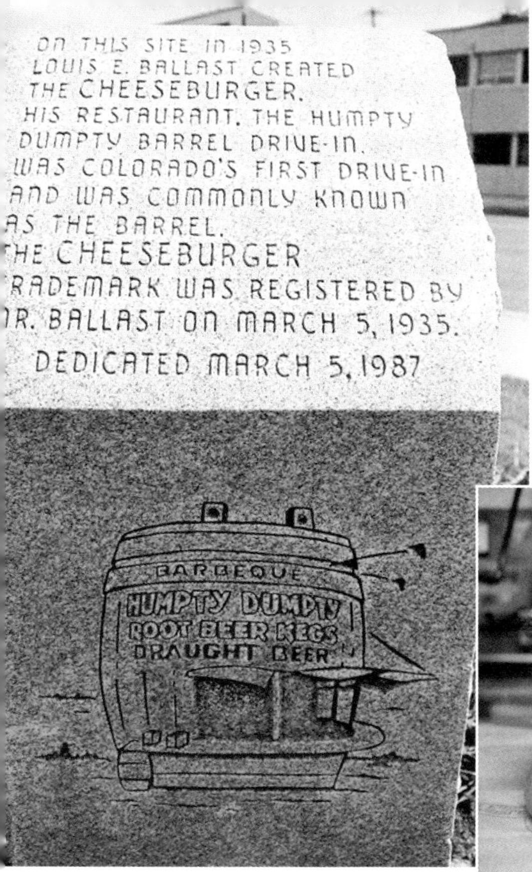

The monument, commemorated in 1987 and now located in a bank parking lot on Speer Boulevard west of downtown Denver, commemorates the alleged invention of the cheeseburger in 1935 by Louis Ballast. Photo by Eric Peterson

A definitively American delicacy, the cheeseburger's origin story has been the subject of controversy over the years. While many people point to Pasadena, California, as its birthplace, a fortuitous copyright brought Denver into the conversation as a possible point of invention. Photo courtesy of Pixabay. https://pixabay.com/photos/cheeseburger-hamburger-bacon-diner-820178

get "cheeseburger" trademarked (he did that in 1935). Despite the trademark, however, he never sued anyone for using it.

The Humpty Dumpty closed in the 1970s and later burned down, but its legacy lives on in the three-foot monument commemorating Ballast's accomplishments. It was installed in 1987 in what is now an otherwise nondescript KeyBank parking lot west of downtown.

THE GATES OF HELL AT THE COURTHOUSE

What happened at the city's seat of power for six straight nights in 1900?

Built in 1883 and demolished in 1933, the Arapahoe County Courthouse served as the city's scales of justice in its early years. It was a grand structure, with ornate stonework, a Renaissance-style cupola, and copper-clad roofs, but it became obsolete when Denver County broke away from Arapahoe County in 1902.

A series of events just before the ink dried on the new county lines also might have helped seal its fateful date with a wrecking ball.

As the story goes, the night janitor was cleaning up one night in 1900 when something phantasmic occurred: The Gates to Hell opened on the second floor, and a horde of supernatural beings wandered the halls from 3 a.m. to daybreak. Then it happened again. And again and again and again. For six consecutive nights, ghosts

"GATES OF HELL" AT THE DENVER COURTHOUSE

What: An alleged interdimensional portal in a long-gone building

Where: Formerly located between 15th and 16th Streets and Court and Tremont Streets downtown

Cost: Free

Pro Tip: For more scary stories about the city, look no further than Dark Side of Denver Ghost Tours.

Before its untimely demise, the Arapahoe County Courthouse had the second-highest dome in the state, second only to the Colorado State Capitol Building.

As seen from the Colorado State Capitol, the since-demolished Arapahoe County Courthouse was an iconic building in the late 1800s and early 1900s, but it disappeared from the city's urban fabric in 1933, more than 30 years after the Gates of Hell allegedly opened here. Photo courtesy of Wikimedia Commons. https://commons.wikimedia.org/wiki/File:Arapahoe_County_Courthouse,_1898.JPG

made themselves at home in the courthouse halls as the aroma of brimstone permeated the air.

Post-demolition, a park, then parking lot, then department store occupied the site, followed by the Sheraton Denver Downtown Hotel that dominates the block today. Ghosts apparently no longer materialize on the second floor of the hotel, but some paranormal investigators claim that there's still a vortex there that offers a conduit between the lands of the living and the dead.

A PEN BIG ENOUGH FOR A PACHYDERM

Were elephants penned in Lower Downtown Denver?

Situated off 15th Street between Blake and Wazee Streets in the heart of what is now known as LoDo (Lower Downtown), the Elephant Corral was a walled-off corral that took up a quarter of a city block.

ELEPHANT CORRAL

What: A super-sized stable that was a hub in Denver's boomtown days

Where: 15th and Wazee Streets

Cost: Free

Pro Tip: The Cherry Creek Trail runs right next to the old Elephant Corral for sightseers on foot or bike.

When entrepreneurs Charles Blake and Andrew Williams opened the facility in 1858, it was home to the biggest buildings in the fledgling boomtown. Its size may have something to do with the moniker, but "seeing the elephant" was Gold Rush–era slang for witnessing something peculiar, which might have had something to do with the name. Another possible origin was an earlier stable of the same name in Iowa. Just like the legends in the Barnum neighborhood on the west side of the city, however, no real elephants ever stomped around here.

Nevertheless, Blake and Williams did brisk business trading teams of oxen for picks and mules for mining when gold-seekers

---

The Elephant Corral came before the common use of currency in Denver, so most business in the early days was done with pinches of gold dust.

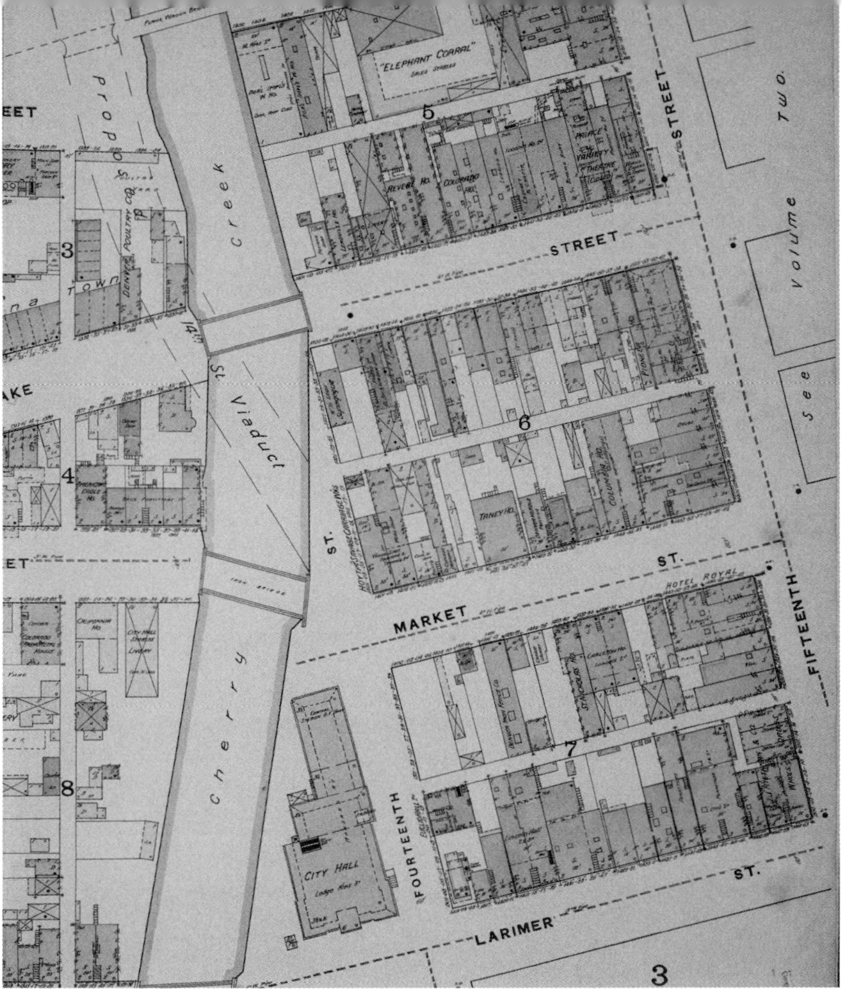

The massive livestock-trading emporium known as the Elephant Corral occupied about a quarter of a city block on the banks of Cherry Creek when gold-seekers arrived en masse in Denver in the late 1850s and 1860s. Photo courtesy of Sanborn Fire Insurance, Wikimedia Commons. https://upload.wikimedia.org/wikipedia/commons/4/4b/Sanborn_Fire_Insurance_Map_from_Denver%2C_Denver_County%2C_Colorado._LOC_sanborn00985_002-6.jpg

arrived. The two also offered lodging, gambling, and other services. The Elephant Corral emerged as one of the first economic and social centers in Denver before a fire destroyed the original corral in 1863. It was swiftly rebuilt, but the property was cleared in the 1880s to make way for new development.

The original structures are no longer standing, but the name is still in use at a mixed-use development on the spot where it once stood.

A DARK NIGHT IN HOP ALLEY

What sparked one of the ugliest events in Denver history?

In the city's early days, Denver was home to a thriving Chinatown centered on Wazee Street.

The Chinese population had risen from four to 238 in the 1870s, and Hop—slang for opium—Alley was dotted with markets, laundries, and other businesses.

On Halloween night in 1880, a bar fight that originally involved only four people spilled into the streets of downtown Denver and escalated into a race riot.

A mob of white residents attacked Chinese residents and burned Denver's Chinatown to the ground. The hateful throng hung one elderly Chinese man, Sing Lee, and then proceeded to hang his body again at a more visible location to make a statement: Chinese people weren't welcome in Denver anymore.

The message was loud and clear, and the city's Chinese population dwindled to about 100 residents in the mid-1900s.

HOP ALLEY

What: Denver's lost Chinatown

Where: Between Wazee and Blake Streets

Cost: Free

Pro Tip: The events of 1880 are memorialized by a plaque at 20th and Blake Streets.

The riot in Denver had a national impact: as it was right before a presidential election, its effects reverberated and paved the way for the Chinese Exclusion Act of 1882.

The plaque mounted near the alley at 20th and Blake Streets is one of the few remaining links to the lost Chinatown in LoDo. It concludes by noting that the tragedy of 1880 did not "end Denver's struggles with the underlying issues of racial prejudice." Photos by Eric Peterson

The rationale for the racially motivated violence is familiar: the whites who committed the acts of terror were largely angry that Chinese people were very good at doing hard work for low pay, with few complaints or questions asked. For some, that was reason enough to commit murder.

THE QUEEN CITY'S BLOWTORCH

Where outside Denver was one of the world's biggest radio towers?

A looming spire east of Denver, the 475-foot-tall structure in Aurora served as the ultra-powerful transmitter for the KOA radio station until its decommissioning in 1959.

The Federal Communications Commission designated KOA a Class I-A radio station, a link in a national network of 50,000-watt transmitters. As a result, General Electric, the station's owner at the time, constructed an ornate, Art Deco-style office in 1932. The company then built what was then the country's tallest self-supported radio tower when it was completed in 1934.

With the upgrade, KOA could broadcast shows to listeners up and down the Rockies from Canada to New Mexico.

With the ability to catapult radio waves hundreds of miles in all directions, these Class I-A stations were known as "blowtorches" or "flamethrowers." It's not hyperbole; the transistor tubes would get so hot that

THE OLD KOA TOWER

What: A giant transmitter that once stood on the plains

Where: 18500 E. Colfax Ave., Aurora

Cost: Free

Pro Tip: The tower site is on Colfax Avenue, known as the longest commercial street in the United States.

The tower was so prominent that local leaders named the nearest street after it: Tower Road.

This aerial photo captures the dramatic scale of the KOA tower shortly after it was built in the 1930s. The 475-foot structure was the tallest self-supported radio tower in the country when GE unveiled it in 1934. Photo courtesy of John Schneider, TheRadioHistorian.org

they needed plenty of water to stave off a meltdown. In Aurora, a decorative fountain out front also served as a cooling pond for the tubes.

While the legendary tower is no longer scraping the sky east of Denver, the City of Aurora designated the historic building (now an office for the Colorado Department of Transportation) a landmark in 2001.

LOST AND FOUND MISSILE SILOS

What happens when the government decommissions a nuclear weapons facility?

There are 11 former federal missile launch complexes on the plains east of Denver: six Titan I and five Atlas E sites. Both varieties were equipped to fire intercontinental ballistic missiles (ICBMs) with atomic payloads halfway around the planet beginning in the early 1960s.

After the facilities were decommissioned in the mid-1960s, the federal government sold them to a variety of public and private owners. One has been converted into a park, others are being used for commercial purposes, and yet others are being converted into private residences.

The missile sites have everything an aspiring supervillain or doomsday prepper would want in a home: plenty of acreage, multiple underground silos, a command center, and a network of connecting tunnels. However, many of them are also polluted with a variety of nasty chemicals; cleanup and remediation is ongoing.

The pollution hasn't stopped a few enterprising individuals from taking on these massive fixer-upper projects: one owner in Kansas converted an Atlas E complex into a "subterra castle" with 47-ton blast doors leading into a cozy but impenetrable abode.

FORMER MISSLE LAUNCH SITES

What: These Cold War relics could be renovated into massive mansions.

Where: Multiple locations east of Denver

Cost: Free

Pro Tip: Missile Site Park outside Greeley (about 60 miles northeast of Denver) offers camping ($20 per day) and tours of the old Atlas E facility by reservation (free).

The Titan I program was only active for three years (1959–1962) before more advanced missiles were developed. The missile (pictured during a test launch) was never used as a weapon of war. The Atlas E had an even shorter shelf life: 1962 to 1964. Photo courtesy of Wikimedia Commons. https://en.m.wikipedia.org/wiki/File:Titan_I_ICBM.jpg

As of early 2020, one Titan I complex (near Bennett, about 30 miles east of Denver) was on the market for $4.2 million. The listing highlighted 50,000 square feet of space on 210 acres, with a half-mile of tunnels. The owners were marketing the Cold War relic as a potential hemp farm.

The Titan I was one of the first ICBMs developed by the United States. With a range of 6,100 miles, the 98-foot missile carried a 3.75-megaton nuclear warhead and was fueled by highly refined kerosene.

THIRTY STORIES OF BRICKS

Where was the tallest smokestack on earth at the dawn of the 20th century?

At 350 feet in height, the Omaha-Grant Smelter smokestack was long the tallest structure in Denver after it was built in 1892, when it was reputedly the tallest smokestack on Earth. With an internal bore that was 30 feet wide and 12-foot-thick walls, the big chimney was said to be made of enough bricks (about 3 million) to build more than 500 houses, and weighed in at a beefy 7,000 tons.

The smokestack emitted gases from the smelter in its shadows, refining gold and silver ore from Colorado's mines. It was only in operation for a little more than a decade, however, thanks to an economic downturn, labor strife, and increasingly obsolete technology. After the smelter shuttered in 1903, the monolithic stack was inactive (aside from the occasional daredevils who

OMAHA-GRANT SMELTER STACK

What: The world's biggest chimney once dominated the Denver skyline.

Where: 41st Street and Brighton Boulevard

Cost: Free

Pro Tip: The stack site is now occupied by the Denver Coliseum and National Western Center, home to the annual National Western Stock Show and Rodeo.

"From its mighty mouth . . . spewed the smoke from rich ores that flowed through its smelter by the millions of tons." – *The Denver Post* (when the Omaha-Grant Smelter stack was demolished).

After smelters near the mines in Leadville, Colorado, and other gold and silver hubs in the state hit capacity, industrialists such as James Benton Grant moved operations to Denver to serve a broader market. Photo courtesy of Wikimedia. https://commons.wikimedia.org/wiki/File:US-CO(1891)_p116_DENVER,_OMAHE_%26_GRANT_SMELTING_WORKS.jpg

DENVER: OMAHA & GRANT SMELTING WORKS.

climbed the internal rungs all the way to the top) but impossible to miss for another 47 years.

That era ended with the demolition of the smokestack on February 25, 1950. It was a big day in Denver. An estimated 250,000 people gathered to watch it come down. The first blasts of dynamite had no effect, so crews rigged more explosives and got most of the job done. The final dynamite blew up the remnants the following day.

ASTEROID RANCH

Where near Denver is the geological record of an asteroid hit captured like a bug in amber?

On the plains east of Denver, the West Bijou Ranch is a paleontologist's dream. It's known to the scientific community as the best spot on the planet to study the K-Pg boundary.

And what is the K-Pg boundary? On the ranch, it's a 1.18-inch band of dark rock that's easy to see in the strata on exposed ground.

More importantly, the K-Pg boundary is the geologic layer that marks the end of the Mesozoic era and the beginning of the Cenozoic. In layman's terms, it's a thin band of rock resulting from the massive asteroid strike that led to a mass extinction, as it separates the dinosaur fossils from those of the creatures that followed.

As the theory goes, a six- to nine-mile wide comet or asteroid struck Earth about 66 million years ago. The impact was the equivalent of several million nuclear weapons detonating at once. Then the dinosaurs died off, and new species evolved to fill the missing links in the food chain.

The 7,500-acre West Bijou Ranch has been dubbed "a mecca" for scientists studying the K-Pg boundary because of how easily visible it is. Here, the thin layer of rock tells a clear story about the planet's past.

West Bijou is a working bison ranch owned by the Savory Institute, a nonprofit dedicated to holistic practices that regenerate grasslands all over the world. Numbering about

---

Due to the unique lens it offers into Earth history, the West Bijou Ranch was designated as a National Natural Landmark by the National Park Service in 2017.

Beyond its paleontological significance, the West Bijou Ranch is a working bison ranch with about 400 of the magnificent beasts roaming its 7,500 acres. Their disturbance of the soil helps sustain the prairie's health. Photo courtesy of Byron Shelton, Savory Institute

400, the bison are a big part of such practices, as their activities help return the prairie to a natural state.

WEST BIJOU RANCH

What: A paleontologist's playground

Where: 60100 E. County Rd. 42, Strasburg (about 31 miles east of Denver)

Cost: Free

Pro Tip: Tours of the ranch are often available by reservation in advance.

DENVER'S PSYCHEDELIC CANINE

Where did numerous rock legends perform in Denver in the late 1960s?

The Denver location of the Family Dog rock club was backed by the founders of Family Dog Productions in San Francisco (which got its start producing immersive rock shows in 1966) and was also known as the Denver Dog. In its 10-month incarnation on West Evans Avenue, a veritable who's who of rock and roll played gigs at the legendary concert hall that opened at the tail end of the "Summer of Love."

It was instantly *the* place for up-and-coming rock stars to play in the Mile High City. In the first month alone, Janis Joplin, the Grateful Dead, the Doors, and Buffalo Springfield took the stage. Other big names on the marquee from its opening in September 1967 to its July 1968 shutdown included Jefferson Airplane, Chuck Berry, Cream, Jimi Hendrix, and Frank Zappa.

It was the first venue from late, great Denver concert promoter Barry Fey, and it was known for its psychedelic posters advertising the shows as well as the mind-bending light shows that complemented the music. The venue's demise was accelerated by zealous Denver police officers who targeted longhaired concertgoers and musicians and made numerous

---

Legendary singer Otis Redding was scheduled to play the Family Dog on December 22, 1967, but the show was canceled after he died in a plane crash two weeks before. His hit song "(Sittin' on) The Dock of the Bay" was released a month later.

Now PT's Showclub, the Family Dog saw performances by Jimi Hendrix, Janis Joplin, Frank Zappa, and the Grateful Dead in its all-too-short life as a music venue on West Evans Avenue. Photo by Eric Peterson

drug busts in the process. Some of the arrested claimed that the drugs were planted on them.

Fey moved on to other venues and ventures, but the Family Dog stands out as a highlight of his contribution to the local concert business. In less than a year, it helped establish Denver as a stop for touring rock acts as it catalyzed the local music scene. Today, the building houses PT's Showclub, a strip joint.

THE FAMILY DOG

What: The club hosted more rock legends in 10 months than most venues do in 10 years.

Where: 1601 W. Evans Ave.

Cost: $10 (PT's cover). Note: This is an adults-only venue with nude dancers.

Pro Tip: Relive the Family Dog's glory days at the nearby Levitt Pavilion, one of the city's newer concert venues in Ruby Hill Park.

JOHN BRISBEN WALKER: A CASTLE AND A DREAM

What park has trails, castle ruins, and the cornerstone of a never-built White House in the West?

About 25 miles southwest of downtown Denver in the foothills of the Rocky Mountains, Mount Falcon Park is part of Jefferson County Open Space.

Spread across grassy meadows and forested mountains, it's one of the easiest hiking areas to access from the city, but several of the park's manmade features are notable as well.

John Brisben Walker owned an early automobile company and *Cosmopolitan Magazine* before moving to Colorado. He was one of Denver's most prominent citizens as a landowner and entrepreneur who ran a steamship on the South Platte River and produced the city's first rodeo.

In 1909, Walker built a castle on Mount Falcon. Dubbed "Falcon Castle," its design was modeled after one of King Ludwig's castles in Bavaria.

But Walker didn't stop there: With a vision for a "Summer White House," he laid a marble cornerstone in 1911 and launched a campaign to raise the funds to build another palatial structure for US presidents to use as a vacation home near his castle. The $300,000 budget (about $8 million in 2020 dollars) proved a stumbling block, however, and the project never got off the drawing board.

MOUNT FALCON OPEN SPACE PARK

What: Hike to a castle and back in an hour or less.

Where: 21074 Mount Falcon Rd., Indian Hills

Cost: Free

Pro Tip: Take the Tower Trail for grand views from a lookout tower and the menacingly named Devil's Elbow (about 3 miles round-trip).

With some of the closest hiking trails to Denver, Mount Falcon Open Space Park offers an easy getaway from the city, as well as a fascinating history owed primarily to one man: John Brisben Walker. Photo courtesy of Creative Commons. https://commons.wikimedia.org/wiki/File:Parmalee_Trail_@_Castle_Trail_2016-07-12_960.jpg

Walker also had plans for what is now Red Rocks Amphitheatre (see p. 74), below Mount Falcon, and even invited a leading opera star, Mary Garden, to sing at the site to demonstrate its legendary acoustics.

But lightning struck (literally!) in 1918, sparking a fire that destroyed the castle, and Brisben returned to the East Coast. The City of Denver bought the amphitheatre from him in 1927, and he passed away in 1931. The surrounding parkland remained private property until 1974.

His castle ruins are still standing, preserved at the end of a 0.7-mile trail, and the hike continues to the cornerstone 0.8 miles away. In all, there are 11 miles of multiuse trails at the park.

After private and public funding failed to materialize for Walker's Summer White House, he proposed another financing concept: a dime from every schoolchild in the United States. That strategy failed as well.

THE GOLDEN CHILD

Where is the largest nugget of gold ever found in Colorado?

On July 23, 1887, Tom Groves and Harry Lytton struck gold in a very big way.

Prospecting near Breckenridge, Colorado, the duo unearthed a 13.5-pound nugget of crystalline gold. Groves swaddled it in a blanket for the trip back into town, and then paraded it around like a baby in the streets after he arrived.

Lytton and Groves sold it to a local businessman for a presumably high price, and the businessman put it on a train for Denver. The owners donated it to what is now the Denver Museum of Nature & Science, and then the mystery begins. The nugget was not seen in public for decades. This was odd, as most superlative mining discoveries made the rounds at the World's Fair and other big events at that time.

Fast-forward more than 80 years from the original discovery of the nugget, and a sleuthing pastor rediscovered Tom's Baby in a bank vault owned by the Denver Museum of Nature & Science in 1972. It was mixed with a number of other artifacts in a crate that had likely been stashed in the vault during World War II.

But the chunk in the vault, while positively identified by people who had seen it firsthand before it went missing, weighed about three pounds less than the original specimen. To this day, it's not clear what happened to the missing gold.

Based on weight alone, Tom's Baby was worth about $250,000 in early 2020 when gold was about $1,500 an ounce, but experts say it's worth much more due to its unique characteristics.

Found at the bottom of a hydrothermal cavity, Tom's Baby is a geological anomaly. Most of the gold found in similar spots is wiry rather than in the form of a massive chunk. Photo courtesy of Creative Commons, James St. John. https://commons.wikimedia.org/wiki/File:Gold_vein_stockwork_in_limonite_(Gold_Flake_Vein,_Farncomb_Hill,_near_Breckenridge,_Colorado,_USA)_3_(17078770851).jpg

Tom's Baby is now on display as the centerpiece of the Coors Gems and Minerals Hall (see p. 172) at the Denver Museum of Nature & Science.

TOM'S BABY

What: The largest mass of gold ever discovered in Colorado

Where: Denver Museum of Nature & Science, 2001 Colorado Blvd.

Cost: Adults, $19.95; seniors, $16.95; children, $14.95

Pro Tip: Plan to spend the better part of a day at the museum, which is also home to a planetarium and IMAX theater and is located in City Park.

STONE FOREST IN ROSEDALE

What landmark halfway across the planet has a counterpart on the south side of Denver?

The capital of the southern Yunnan province in China, Kunming is one of Denver's 13 sister cities. The relationship stems from World War II history: Kunming was the base for the Flying Tigers, a group of pilots from the US Air Force, Navy, and Marines who flew planes with Chinese colors against Japan. One of the Flying Tigers, the late John Yee, moved to Denver after the war and was instrumental in cultivating the sister-city relationship.

Located at the foot of the Himalayas, Kunming (pop. 6.7 million) is also known as the gateway to the Stone Forest (or Shilin), named for upright limestone formations, also known as karst, that jut from the earth like aboveground stalagmites.

To cement the status of sister cities, Kunming leaders had several of the karst "trees" shipped about 7,000 miles to Denver for a display atop City of Kunming

CITY OF KUNMING PARK

What: Limestone pillars mark one of Denver's sister cities.

Where: 200 East Harvard Ave.

Cost: Free

Pro Tip: Situated on a hillside, the park is one of the best places to watch the sunset or Fourth of July fireworks in Denver.

Like Denver, Kunming is a mile-high city. Actually, it's a bit higher than a mile, at 6,200 feet above sea level.

The capital of Yunnan province in southwestern China, Kunming is known as the gateway to the otherworldly Stone Forest, or Shilin. The "trees" are actually limestone formations known as karst. Photo courtesy of Creative Commons, CEphoto, Uwe Aranas. https://commons.wikimedia.org/wiki/File:Shilin_Yunnan_China_Shilin-Stone-Forest-01.jpg

Inset: City of Kunming Park. Photo courtesy of Eric Peterson

Park in the Rosedale neighborhood in the southern reaches of the city. The distinctive ring of stone pillars brings a little piece of the Stone Forest to Denver.

Situated on a treed hill, the block-sized park, ringed by houses in a peaceful neighborhood, is a favorite of mindful meditators, martial artists, and dog walkers.

SNOOZING SLIDE

Where in Denver can children climb on a slumbering subterranean buckaroo?

For decades, the playground at Bear Creek Park in southwestern Denver was dominated by a singular purple sombrero for children to climb up and slide down. The distinctive concrete attraction was beloved as a local landmark by kids who grew up in the neighborhood.

When the park got an upgrade in the 2000s, locals naturally did not want to see the big hat meet its doom on the business end of a bulldozer and lobbied for its preservation. The landscape architects who designed the new playground ultimately agreed it needed to stay, and adapted the sombrero slide into their new concept for the old playground.

The hat now sheathes the unseen head of a sleeping giant cowboy, complete with two knees and one super-sized boot peeking out of the ground where kids are likewise welcome to play. Adjacent panels tell the story of the big fella's adventures.

SLEEPING GIANT COWBOY PLAYGROUND

What: Public art that kids can play on

Where: 3550 S. Raleigh St.

Cost: Free

Pro Tip: Families should pack a picnic lunch and make an afternoon of their visit.

The park is located about three miles west of the South Platte River on the Bear Creek Trail for bicyclists and pedestrians.

As the tall tale goes, a great, big cowboy wanted to take a break from his rustling and found just the spot for a nap on the north bank of Bear Creek. Kids playing on his hat don't rouse him at all. Photo by Eric Peterson

Apparently, the leviathan cowpoke thought this spot next to Bear Creek was as good a spot as any to burrow in for a nap, and he's been snoozing here ever since.

The project also added a number of colorful new features to the playground area, including a treehouse, an amphitheater, horseshoe pits, and a buried time capsule.

DENVER'S FALSE START

Where was the first permanent pioneer settlement on the South Platte River?

During the Pikes Peak Gold Rush of 1858—and just a month before Auraria was established near present-day downtown Denver about five miles to the north—a group of prospectors built three rows of cabins on the east bank of the South Platte River near its confluence with Little Dry Creek. Its founders named the fledgling town Montana City after the Spanish word for "mountain" and panned for gold in the river's waters.

While trappers and prospectors had previously pitched tents in the vicinity, the cabins were the first permanent structures inside what are now Denver city limits.

Then part of Kansas Territory, Montana City had a notably brief existence. The search for gold in the South Platte proved fruitless, and the population quickly dwindled. The cabins were dismantled by winter and rebuilt downstream in Auraria as that settlement gained steam before it merged with Denver in 1860.

MONTANA CITY

What: The first permanent settlement in what is now Denver was short-lived.

Where: 2300 South Platte River Dr.

Cost: Free

Pro Tip: Bring a pan and try your hand at prospecting the river for gold.

The old Montana City site is on the Greenway Trail, which follows the South Platte River for about 30 miles through the Denver metro area.

A replica of a covered wagon (minus the cover) commemorates the notably temporary settlement of Montana City about five miles south of downtown Denver on the South Platte River. Photo by Eric Peterson

The ghost town site is now Grant-Frontier Park on the south side of Denver, with river access, picnic tables, and a nifty playground for kids. The long-gone settlement is memorialized in the form of a wagon, a cabin replica, and a plaque, but Montana City is otherwise a largely forgotten chapter in the Denver history book.

A THRILLING TIME CAPSULE

What is the only operating White City amusement park on Earth?

In the early 1900s, dozens of amusement parks owed their inspiration—and name—to White City at the 1893 World's Columbian Exposition in Chicago.

Named for its white stucco structures and bright lighting, that original (and temporary) White City in Chicago was the forefather of the modern amusement park and included a mile-long midway, the original Ferris wheel, and an early version of a roller coaster.

More than 30 White City parks subsequently operated in the early 20th century in the United States, as well as in Canada, the United Kingdom, and Australia. A century later, they are largely forgotten, and nearly all of them have shut down.

All but one, that is: Lakeside Amusement Park on the northwest edge of Denver. The park opened as White City in 1908 and continues to operate every summer with a number of notably historic rides and attractions, including a Parker carousel that started spinning at the park in 1908, a steam-powered train from the 1904 St. Louis World's Fair, and the Cyclone, a wooden-rail roller coaster that dates to 1940. The landmark Tower of Jewels was a standard feature of the White City parks.

Lakeside is its own municipality just west of the Denver city limits at Sheridan Boulevard, with its own police department and city government. As of 2010, the population was eight, making it Colorado's least populous community.

This aerial photograph of Lakeside Amusement Park, taken in the 1960s, shows off the Cyclone roller coaster (center), the Tower of Jewels (center, below the Cyclone), and Lake Rhoda (left). Photo courtesy of Creative Commons, Robert Boser, EditorASC. https://commons.wikimedia.org/wiki/File:Lakeside_Amusement_Park,_1966.jpg

Photo by Eric Peterson

The park got an Art Deco update in the 1930s and is known today for its eye-catching neon signs. Over the years, many historic rides have been decommissioned but remain as monuments to the thrills gone by. The best thing about Lakeside? As Denver changes and changes, it has kept things pretty much the same.

LAKESIDE AMUSEMENT PARK

What: The last White City standing

Where: 4601 Sheridan Blvd., Lakeside

Cost: $17 to $27 for unlimited rides, or $3.50 gate admission and ticketed rides

Pro Tip: If you don't have much time, stop by for a few of the more historic rides; you can buy individual tickets instead of an unlimited pass.

FIRST AMENDMENT LANDMARK

Where is the oldest press club in the United States?

In downtown Denver, the Denver Press Club is the oldest continually operating organization of its kind in the country. The club first met in 1867, and it formally incorporated a decade later as the Denver Press Club after Colorado became a state.

The club met in the basement of a grocery store on Larimer Street in the early years, but it eventually outgrew that space and moved into new digs that are still in use today. Built in 1925 for $50,000, the handsome clubhouse in downtown Denver features a restaurant and bar on the ground level, an event venue upstairs, and a billiards room in the basement.

The clubhouse has been graced by numerous presidents as well as journalists of renown ranging from Damon Runyon to Molly Ivins to Jimmy Breslin to Bob Woodward. It was designated a historic landmark by the Denver Landmark Preservation Commission in 1986 and added to the National Register of Historic Places in 2017.

DENVER PRESS CLUB

What: The oldest active press club in the United States

Where: 1330 Welton St.

Cost: Free

Pro Tip: The bar here is open to the public, as are numerous special events.

The First Amendment to the United States Constitution, guaranteeing freedom of speech, is front and center on a plaque that is bolted at the entrance.

The second building occupied by the Denver Press Club, the oldest such organization in the nation, has housed the club downtown since 1925. The two-story structure was added to the National Register of Historic Places in 2017. Photo courtesy of Creative Commons, Jeffrey Beall. https://commons.wikimedia.org/wiki/File:Denver_Press_Club_(31858188114).jpg

Of special note is a wall clad in caricatures of local journalism fixtures and a mural by Herndon Davis, one of the foremost practitioners of the form and best known for his "The Face on the Bar Room Floor" in the mining boomtown of Central City, Colorado, west of Denver. His 1945 work at the Denver Press Club captures a newsroom in all its glory, with a who's who of local journalists of the era.

PHANTOM RACETRACK

Where was the auto racing mecca of Denver during the sport's 1950s heyday?

If you listen closely, you might just hear the roar of ghost hot rods zooming by on a quiet night.

This one-fifth-mile oval track on the northwestern edge of Denver is a thing of legend for car nuts. It was the place to go for auto racing from 1938 to 1988, with a pause during World War II. It was so popular that the first postwar race drew 11,000 spectators to a venue with a capacity of 7,000, and the sport enjoyed a heyday with an uptick in attendance in the 1950s.

After promoting several races on a dirt track at the same location, Ben Krasner built the paved speedway as a complement to Lakeside Amusement Park, which he also owned, just to the north. The track was 75 percent encircled by seating, with the main grandstand on the west side, topped by the announcer's booth. A who's who of racing legends circled the oval over the years of the track's operation.

LAKESIDE SPEEDWAY

What: Denver's ghost racetrack

Where: 15401 West 44th Ave., Lakeside

Cost: Free

Pro Tip: Take a gander at the track from the Lakeside Amusement Park parking lot to see the old gearhead mecca.

Old Lakeside Speedway fans and racers have been pushing for a memorial or museum at the long-shuttered track.

The Lakeside Speedway was one of the most popular venues for auto racing in the Rockies from the 1930s to the 1980s. Since its closure in 1988, nature has slowly overtaken the old oval in the form of overgrowth. Photo by Eric Peterson

A spectator fatality in 1988 led to the end of racing at Lakeside. While it hasn't hosted a race in decades, the speedway still exists, but the track is overgrown with foliage, and the structure is suspect. Rumors of its demolition have been rampant in recent years, but the wrecking ball has yet to arrive.

THE BARON'S COW PALACE

Where was livestock-tinged air used as a cure for tuberculosis?

In the Montclair neighborhood in northeast Denver, Baron Walter von Richthofen, the uncle of World War I German flying ace nicknamed the Red Baron, built a castle as his home in 1887. Inspired by Prussian architecture, Richthofen Castle was the centerpiece of his vision for Montclair, Denver's first streetcar-served suburb, which also included a high-end health resort. In those days, the castle was hard to miss: the turreted structure, sheathed in rhyolite quarried from the town of Castle Rock about 25 miles south of Denver, totaled 14,600 square feet with 35 rooms on an acre of land.

RICHTHOFEN CASTLE AND THE MOLKEREI

What: A castle and a barn-turned-sanatorium are now landmarks in east Denver.

Where: 12th Avenue and Pontiac Street

Cost: Free

Pro Tip: Montclair Park also features swimming pools, horseshoe pits, and tennis courts.

However, von Richthofen only lived in his castle for a few years before he began traveling the world with his wife, Louise, and he passed away in 1898. The castle has changed hands several times in the years since, with various owners renovating and modifying it and selling off most of the surrounding land. It is now a private residence.

Built by von Richthofen as a barn in 1888, the adjacent Molkerei (German for "milk house") later became a sanatorium for tuberculosis patients who flocked to Denver under advisement that the thin air and dry climate would be good for their health. The cows remained at the Molkerei after its

In the early 20th century, the castle's second owner, Denver manufacturing tycoon Edwin Hendrie, added a west wing and south wing, while adding Tudor elements to the Prussian-inspired exterior. Photo courtesy of Creative Commons, Craig Talbert. https://en.wikipedia.org/wiki/Richthofen_Castle#/media/File:Richthofen_Castle_(48854821156).jpg

conversion to a health-care facility, and the beds were situated above their stables. The aroma and fresh milk were dubiously rumored to offer relief from the disease.

The Molkerei is now the Montclair Civic Building, an event venue and community center in Montclair Park, and is open to the public.

WASH PARK DREAMING

What's the significance of the statue of three children in a shoe in Washington Park?

Eugene Field was the Dr. Seuss of his day. In the late 1800s, he wrote fantastical children's poems that captured the imagination of a generation and earned him the nickname "The Poet of Childhood."

Among Field's best-known works, his 1889 poem "Wynken, Blynken, and Nod" was an ode to dreaming. It tells the tale of three children who go sailing one night in oversized footwear, converse with the Moon, and cast fishing nets among the stars.

It begins: "Wynken, Blynken, and Nod one night / sailed off in a wooden shoe / Sailed on a river of crystal light / into a sea of dew / 'Where are you going, and what do you wish?' the old moon asked the three / 'We have come to fish for the herring fish / that live in this beautiful sea!'"

By the end of the poem, the stellar anglers return to their beds in time to wake in the morning.

"Wynken, Blynken, and Nod" was just one of many popular children's poems written by Field, who lived in Denver in the early 1880s before going on to greater prominence in Chicago.

His Mile High City home on Colfax Avenue was moved to Washington Park, where Mabel Landrum Torrey's 1918 sculpture of the dream trio memorializes their star-fishing trip in the night sky.

Sculptor Mabel Landrum Torrey was born in 1886 in a sod house in northeastern Colorado. Her marble *Wynken, Blynken, and Nod* statue, originally installed in a fountain in Washington Park, was her first major commission and is considered her most prominent work.

Wynken, Blynken, and Nod weren't just the protagonists in a Eugene Field poem; they also made appearances in a Disney cartoon in 1938 and later in a song popularized by Carly Simon and her sister, Lucy. Photo courtesy of Creative Commons, Matt Wright. https://en.m.wikipedia.org/wiki/File:2006-03-30_Wynken.jpg

WYNKEN, BLYNKEN, AND NOD STATUE

What: A monument to childhood dreams

Where: Exposition Avenue and Franklin Street in Washington Park

Cost: Free

Pro Tip: Washington Park is one of Denver's most popular parks, featuring a pair of lakes, boat and bike rentals, croquet courts, and other diversions.

RADIOACTIVE STREETS

Why did some of Denver's streets become part of an environmental cleanup project?

Radium was big in Denver in the early 1900s.

After Marie and Pierre Curie successfully isolated radium in Paris 1898, the element was in high demand for medical applications, many of which proved to be scientifically dubious. Colorado's mines were especially productive, and Denver became an international hub for the fledgling industry in the early 20th century.

The city was home to a number of companies involved in the mining, milling, and processing of radium, including the Shattuck Chemical Company on the south side of Denver.

The boom was short-lived, but it left a lasting mark. In the late 1970s, the then-nascent Environmental Protection Agency (EPA) started testing the soil at some of the former homes of radium-related businesses and found a lot of them were radioactive.

For the next three decades, the Denver Radium Superfund Site involved the cleanup of 65 different sites in and around Denver. That number included a number of streets. Leftover ore was often used to pave streets, leaving them notably radioactive. Many of the streets were excavated entirely and rebuilt, and the rubble was shipped out of state.

Down at the Shattuck site, the cleanup was considered complete after the property was capped with a concrete

---

Some streets with low-level radioactivity were deemed safe by the EPA, as they were buried under several repavings of asphalt.

This advertisement, printed in the Journal of the Medical Society of New Jersey *in 1922, is emblematic of the public perception of Colorado's radium industry in its heyday. The radioactive element was considered to be a medical miracle by many before its negative health impacts became known. Photo courtesy of Internet Archive Book Images,* Journal of the Medical Society of New Jersey. *https://www.flickr.com/photos/126377022@N07/14803616383*

monolith, but its neighbors were none too happy when tests revealed the radioactivity was not entirely contained. A more intensive cleanup commenced, officially completed in 2006, and the property is now home to a slick new apartment complex.

RADIOACTIVE STREETS

What: Denver was paved (in part) with radium.

Where: Multiple locations, including the Shattuck site at West Colorado Avenue and South Bannock Street

Cost: Free

Pro Tip: Don't worry about this when you visit; the EPA deemed the cleanup complete and the streets safe in 2006.

FLOOD OF THE CENTURY

What happened after the biggest flood in Denver's history?

The South Platte River runs through Denver, both geographically and historically. The city was founded on its banks in the late 1850s and mushroomed on either side of it for more than a century without a major incident.

THE 1965 FLOOD

What: The South Platte River's 100-year flood led to a restoration push.

Where: Citywide

Cost: Free

Pro Tip: The best way to see the South Platte River and the post-flood restoration and recreation projects is via the Greenway Trail, which follows the river for about 30 miles through metro Denver.

Then came the flood of June 1965. A torrential thunderstorm to the south of Denver overwhelmed the river's tributaries and then the river itself. The city was quickly inundated on June 16 when the river's flow hit 150,000 cubic feet per second; 300 was normal.

It was a 100-year disaster: all manner of debris washed into the streets, 21 people died, and statewide property damage topped $500 million, or more than $4 billion in today's dollars. A new dam created Chatfield Reservoir to prevent a repeat occurrence.

The silver lining? The city got serious about cleaning up the river, establishing a committee that later became the nonprofit

---

A memorial in South Platte Park in Littleton features metallic waves at the 15-foot mark where the floodwaters peaked in 1965.

The South Platte River normally flows at a rate of about 300 cubic feet per second. On June 16, 1965, the flow hit 500 times that rate: 150,000 cubic feet per second. Photo by Eric Peterson

Greenway Foundation. In the 1970s, the foundation's first projects were Confluence Park (featuring the first urban whitewater park on the planet), Globeville Landing Park, and a riverside trail between the two. More trails and parks were built in the decades since, as pollution decreased and fish and wildlife populations rebounded.

The project emerged as a national model. The city has enjoyed an estimated $10 billion return on a $100 million investment into environmental and recreational infrastructure on the river.

FIVE POINTS' HOUSE OF JAZZ

Where was the swingingest jazz club in the "Harlem of the West?"

Opening as the Baxter Hotel in 1912 and renamed the Rossonian in 1929, the triangular, Beaux Arts-style landmark in the Five Points neighborhood earned a reputation as the spot to catch some of the best live music in Denver.

The best of the best jazz legends took to the stage at the Rossonian Lounge in the subsequent decades, including Count Basie, Dinah Washington, Nat King Cole, Ella Fitzgerald, and Duke Ellington. These African American musicians often would play at another hotel in then-segregated Denver, where they were refused lodging, and then perform a later set at the hotel in the African American neighborhood of Five Points, also known as "The Harlem of the West."

Word got out that the old hotel was home to the hottest jazz club between St. Louis and Los Angeles, and the crowds

THE ROSSONIAN HOTEL AND LOUNGE

What: A jazz hotspot from another era

Where: 2642 Welton St.

Cost: Free

Pro Tip: The music could come back as a group of investors is planning to restore the Rossonian Hotel and its legendary lounge.

The hotel was renamed the Rossonian in the 1920s after its African American manager at the time: A. W. L. Ross.

The Rossonian Hotel is located just northeast of downtown Denver on Welton Street, the main thoroughfare through historic Five Points. It owes its triangular shape to one of the five-pointed intersections that gave the neighborhood its name. Photo courtesy of Creative Commons, Jeffrey Beall. https://commons.wikimedia.org/wiki/File:Rossonian_Hotel.JPG

followed. White patrons came to outnumber the African Americans in the audience by the end of the lounge's heyday.

With segregation on the wane, African American entertainers had more lodging options in the wake of World War II, and the star power at the Rossonian dimmed a bit. The hotel and lounge entered a period of underutilization beginning in the 1960s, and the city ultimately foreclosed on the property in 1998, just three years after it was listed on the National Register of Historic Places.

A LITTLE SAIGON IN DENVER

Where is the urban mosaic of Denver most dazzlingly diverse?

In the early 1970s, there wasn't a single Vietnamese grocery store in Denver. That changed with the arrival of refugees from Vietnam after the Vietnam War.

The first Vietnamese market opened on South Federal Boulevard, the primary north–south thoroughfare in west Denver, and other Vietnamese-owned businesses followed. Staples such as Vietnamese noodles, rice paper, and fish sauce became readily available.

The critical mass of Denver's community attracted more and more transplants, and there are now about 40,000 people of Vietnamese descent living in Colorado, many of them in the South Federal Boulevard corridor on the west side of Denver.

In the early 1980s, developers transformed a mobile home park at Alameda Avenue and Federal into the Far East Center, a two-story shopping center with pagoda-inspired architecture and numerous Vietnamese shops, businesses, and restaurants.

Today there are dozens of Vietnamese businesses along South Federal, including a number of grocery stores. The Little Saigon Business District along South Federal between Alameda and Mississippi Avenues was officially established in early 2014.

LITTLE SAIGON

What: The place to go for pho and noodles

Where: South Federal Boulevard between Alameda and Mississippi Avenues

Cost: Varies by restaurant

Pro Tip: Have a meal at one of the many eateries: Pho 96, Golden Pho & Grill, and the Ba Le sandwich shop and bakery are all popular.

The sign at the southern boundary of the Little Saigon Business District at Federal Boulevard and Mississippi Avenue marks the place to go in Denver for Vietnamese food and culture. Photo by Eric Peterson

There is an ongoing push to renovate storefronts and improve streetscaping, as well as an initiative for a southward expansion of the business district four blocks to Florida Avenue. Leaders even have a vision for a clock tower modeled on the distinctive oversized timepiece atop Cho Ben Thanh Market in Saigon, or Ho Chi Minh City.

VietFest is an annual celebration in the Little Saigon Business District to commemorate Tet, the Vietnamese New Year, in February.

THE SPIDER MAN OF DENVER

Why was this arachnid person anything but a hero?

Theodore Edward Coneys graduated from drifter to killer when he murdered Philip Peters in 1941.

Coneys had stopped by Peters's home in northwest Denver to ask for some financial help, but broke in when he realized the home was empty. He hid in the attic when Peters returned home, and lived there secretly for a few weeks. Peters eventually discovered Coneys, who bludgeoned him to death in response.

The neighbors discovered Peters's body the next day. To evade the police, Coneys stuck with his curious hiding place at the scene of the crime. He lived out of sight in the attic and only came down to the house at night.

Peters's wife was in the hospital at the time of the crime. After she returned home, her housekeeper became convinced the house was haunted, and both of them moved out to avoid a confrontation with the undead.

About nine full months after the murder, the police

THE SPIDER MAN OF DENVER

What: He was no superhero.

Where: 3335 West Moncrieff Pl.

Cost: Free

Pro Tip: Don't bother the current residents; they were not involved in Coneys's crimes.

The house remains standing in Denver's trendy West Highland neighborhood today, but without any obvious links to the nefarious happenings that took place there in the early 1940s.

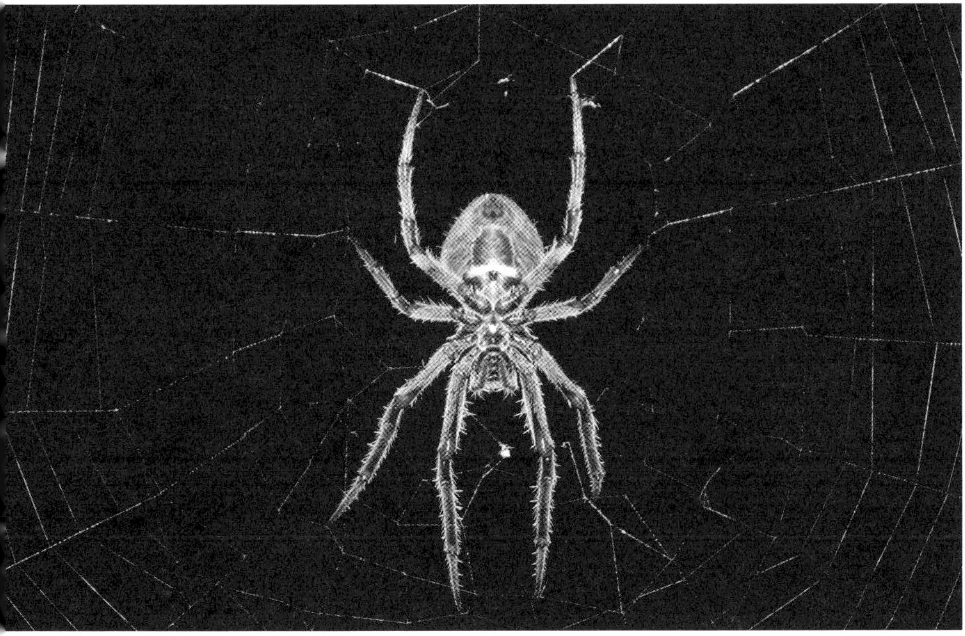

A drifter whose desperation led him to a life of crime in Denver, Theodore Edward Coneys lived in the shadows like a spider and inspired later TV writers with his macabre tale. Photo courtesy of Cesar Agusto Ramirez Vallejo, Pixabay

nabbed Coneys on a routine stop, and he confessed to his crime. The subsequent newspaper coverage nicknamed him as Denver's "Spider Man," when Peter Parker (the alter ego of Marvel Comics' Spider-Man) was but a glimmer in creator Stan Lee's mind. Coneys ended up with a life sentence, and the sensational story later inspired the writers of episodes of *CSI* and *The Simpsons*.

A BASEBALL DIAMOND

Where can you see—and touch—artifacts from baseball's classic parks?

Located a block from Coors Field in LoDo (home of Major League Baseball's Colorado Rockies), the National Ballpark Museum highlights the 14 classic ballparks built between 1909 and 1925, including lost gems such as Ebbets Field in Brooklyn, Shibe Park in Philadelphia, and Tiger Stadium in Detroit. Only two of the parks (Fenway Park in Boston and Chicago's Wrigley Field) are still standing as Major League venues today.

The museum showcases the world-class collection of Bruce Hellerstein, who has pursued artifacts from these historic ballparks for most of his life. Each park has its own exhibit, featuring authentic turnstiles, bases, bricks, usher uniforms, pennants and souvenirs, and programs from its heyday. It's a hands-on museum where you are welcome to pick up and examine many of the artifacts.

A number of the objects on display are rare, or even one of a kind, including a vintage Chicago Cubs on-deck circle from Wrigley Field, a section of the infamous "Green Monster" from Fenway Park, and New York Yankees legend Babe Ruth's 1932 tax form, when he made $76,802.94.

The museum also has an exhibit dedicated to the local minor-league Denver Bears (later renamed the Denver Zephyrs), who played at three home fields in the city: Bears Stadium (later known as Mile High Stadium), west of downtown off Colfax

---

Smithsonian Books once ranked the 1,000-artifact trove held by the National Ballpark Museum among the top 21 baseball collections on Earth.

Just steps from Coors Field in Lower Downtown, the National Ballpark Museum showcases the 14 classic stadiums from baseball's early years, with a second focus on baseball in Denver. Photo courtesy of Steve Crecelius, WonderWorks Studios. www.ballparkmuseum.com

Avenue; Broadway Park (a.k.a. Athletic Park) at Broadway and 7th Avenue; and Merchants Park at Broadway and Dakota Avenue.

NATIONAL BALLPARK MUSEUM

What: Museum dedicated to 14 classic ballparks from the early 1900s

Where: 1940 Blake St.

Cost: Adults, $10; seniors, $5; children, free

Pro Tip: Schedule a visit in tandem with a tour of Coors Field just down the street.

FOOTHILLS FORTRESS

What's the history of this Scottish-style castle south of Denver?

A real estate tycoon from Boston, Charles Alfred Johnson moved to Denver in 1891 and earned a reputation for developing the city's Park Hill neighborhood.

In 1924, Johnson and his wife, Alice Gifford Phillips, decided they wanted to get out of the city and bought the 2,380-acre Flower Homestead property near Sedalia for $5 an acre. Their plan for a modest seasonal lodge snowballed into a vision for a Scottish-style castle as a year-round home.

Renowned architect Burnham Hoyt took cues from castles built in Scotland in the 1450s and designed a majestic 10,000-square-foot structure with 24 rooms and a commanding location on one of the property's bluffs.

For two years, a team of 30 Cornish masons built the castle from local stone and petrified wood. The final product featured all the trappings one would expect to see at a castle: towers, turrets, gargoyles, a great hall with a minstrel balcony, and eight fireplaces.

Originally named Charlford Castle after Johnson and Phillips's sons, Charlie and Gifford, Cherokee Castle was given its modern moniker by the subsequent owner, Mildred Montague Genevieve "Tweet" Kimball, who bought it from Johnson in 1954.

The modern ranch is part of a 12,000-acre open space complex that encompasses an active cattle operation and a wildlife sanctuary with mule deer, black bears, and mountain lions.

Looking out over 12,000 acres of open space, Cherokee Castle drew inspiration from Scotrish castles built in the 15th century. The end result is a stunning 10,000-square-foot structure with 24 rooms. Photo by Nick Lucey, courtesy of James Holmes

Kimball expanded the ranching operations on the property and established the Cherokee Ranch and Castle Foundation before passing away in 1999. Today the foundation offers castle and ranch tours and manages the castle as a venue for special events.

CHEROKEE CASTLE

What: A vision from 15th-century Scotland sits 20 miles south of Denver.

Where: 6113 North Daniels Park Rd., Sedalia

Cost: $20 for castle tours

Pro Tip: Check the website (www.cherokeeranch.org) for the current calendar of events.

DENIZENS OF THE DIORAMA

What magical beings are hiding at the Denver Museum of Nature & Science?

The dioramas at the Denver Museum of Nature & Science depict scenes in places ranging from the Rocky Mountains to Mars. While these spots might not seem like prime elf habitat, it's important to keep your eyes open nonetheless.

Kent Pendleton, the Colorado-based artist behind many of the murals that provide a backdrop to the dioramas, started a tradition by hiding eight elves in his paintings in the early 1970s. At first, it was his own little secret. He painted his first one mistakenly thinking he would be the only person who would notice it.

That was not the case, as the museum has since taken Pendleton's idea and run with it, inserting elven figurines into all sorts of nooks and crannies in the building. A good look at the dioramas of pronghorn, white-tailed deer, or the Hoh Rain Forest in Washington's Olympic National Park rarely goes unrewarded, but many of the little pixies are notably hard to spot.

There is some argument as to whether they're elves, gnomes, or leprechauns. Pendleton has said he started out with leprechauns in mind, but his style evolved into a more elf-like creature.

It's not just elves hiding at the Denver Museum of Nature & Science; eagle-eyed visitors have spotted unicorns, angels, and even Yoda from the *Star Wars* movies hiding among the exhibits.

This brave elf is riding on the back of an Ornithomimus dinosaur in the background of the Cretaceous Creekbed diorama in the Denver Museum of Nature & Science's Prehistoric Journey section. Photo courtesy of Creative Commons, oddharmonic. https://www.flickr.com/photos/oddharmonic/8560499713

His work is also on display at the nearby Denver Zoo as well as in museums in New Mexico, South Carolina, and Wyoming, where you might likewise see some fairy folk hiding in plain sight.

HIDDEN ELVES AT THE DENVER MUSEUM OF NATURE & SCIENCE

What: An artist's secret has snowballed into a museum tradition.

Where: Denver Museum of Nature & Science, 2001 Colorado Blvd.

Cost: Adults, $19.95; seniors, $16.95; children, $14.95

Pro Tip: Patrons can participate in scavenger hunts to find all the elves lurking in the museum. Ask for an elf checklist at the information desk.

ROCKY MOUNTAIN MARDI GRAS

What are the origins of the foodie festival known as A Taste of Colorado?

The Slaves of the Silver Serpent, a secret society of sorts in 19th-century Denver, was looking for ways to spark the local economy after the silver crash of 1893. Their solution? A "Mardi Gras of the West," featuring numerous parades, costume parties, and games.

Denver hosted the first Festival of Mountain and Plain in October 1895. A promotional flyer described the event as a "half week of rare pleasure is planned in connection with the greater object of illustrating to the world Colorado's high standing as an agricultural, mineral and horticultural State."

It was a hit. Some parades drew in excess of 100,000 people with bizarre floats featuring all manner of monsters and deities. A newspaper described one parade in a headline, "Beautiful Designs, Grotesque Figures, Fancy Costumes."

FESTIVAL OF MOUNTAIN AND PLAIN

What: The city partied like it was 1899.

Where: Citywide

Cost: Free

Pro Tip: Check the concert schedule for the free live music at A Taste of Colorado.

After its one-off comebacks in the early 1900s, the festival was resurrected as A Taste of Colorado, a culinary event held on Labor Day weekend in Civic Center Park.

FLOAT OF THE SILVER SERPENT, MYSTIC SPIRIT OF THE GREAT FESTIVAL

This menacing, serpentine float pays homage to the Slaves of the Silver Serpent, the secret society that came up with the Festival of Mountain and Plain after the silver bust in 1893. Photo credit: Public Domain from Colorado Magazine *July 1948. https://www.historycolorado.org/sites/default/files/media/document/2018/ColoradoMagazine_v25n4_July1948.pdf*

In the heart of Denver, Civic Center Park was a primary venue for the festival, with a hulking grandstand for spectators. The coronation of the Queen of the Slaves of the Silver Serpent was a highlight, involving a crown of silver snakes.

After annual festivals from 1895 to 1899 (and one-year revivals in 1901 and 1912), the Festival of Mountain and Plain went bust, and the Slaves of the Silver Serpent slithered into the history books.

WE ALL SCREAM FOR ICE CORES!

Why is there a massive freezer in a Denver suburb with ice samples from all over the world?

Located just west of Denver at the Federal Center in Lakewood, the National Science Foundation Ice Core Facility (NSF-ICF) has the world's largest collection of ice cores available to researchers.

Ice cores are cylindrical samples drilled from glaciers and ice fields all over the world. The lab describes them as "frozen time capsules." Scientists analyze samples from the cores for various research efforts, most of which focus on understanding the past climate states of the Earth.

The NSF-ICF collection includes more than 22,000 meters of ice cores from Antarctica, Greenland, and North America in all. The facility's primary freezer is big (55,000 cubic feet) and cold: the cores are stored at a temperature of 36 degrees below zero Celsius.

The cores are stored in metallic tubes on shelves in the freezer. When a scientist requests a sample, staffers at the NSF-ICF take it to a slightly warmer (24 degrees below zero Celsius) room to meticulously cut a piece from the core and ship it to the scientist's lab.

The largest ice core at the facility is from the West Antarctic Ice Shield Divide project, measuring a whopping 3,405 meters

---

Like tree rings, the layers in ice cores correspond to years and seasons, providing scientists with detailed climate data over hundreds of thousands of years.

In a massive freezer outside Denver, ice cores are stored on shelves in one-meter sections that are retrieved for processing when a scientist requests a sample. Photo courtesy of Wikimedia Commons. https://commons.wikimedia.org/wiki/File:NICL_Freezer.jpg

in length (more than two miles). Scientists are using it to track changing levels of greenhouse gases and climatic shifts over the past 68,000 years.

NATIONAL SCIENCE FOUNDATION ICE CORE FACILITY

What: A huge freezer dedicated to climate science

Where: One Denver Federal Center, Lakewood

Cost: Free

Pro Tip: Tours are available, but they must be scheduled several months in advance on the lab's website (www.icecores.org).

EGGS MARK THE SPOT

What is the egg dish that's most associated with the Mile High City?

On an otherwise standard sidewalk downtown, a dozen "All Things Colorado" plaques dig into some of the legends and lore of the Centennial State. One of them examines the history of one of the definitive local recipes: the Denver omelet.

It starts off with a recipe: "Beat 2-3 eggs per person in a large mixing bowl. Add chopped ham or bacon, green pepper and onion to taste. Pour mixture into a hot frying pan. Fold to form omelet." (Many critics argue that a Denver omelet is not a Denver omelet without cheese, but that's not the only issue.)

The plaque continues, "The Denver omelet was developed to mask the stale flavor of eggs shipped by wagon freight."

Historians have poked holes in this origin story, noting that green peppers were not easy to come by in Colorado in the 19th century. Many observers say the original Denver omelets were served between two pieces of bread in a sandwich format.

DENVER OMELET PLAQUE

What: The history of the definitive local egg dish is a bit unclear.

Where: California Street between 15th and 16th Streets

Cost: Free

Pro Tip: Get your omelet smothered in green chile stew, a Southwestern delicacy.

You can order up a Denver omelet of your own at landmark diner Sam's No. 3, located three blocks from the plaque at 1500 Curtis St.

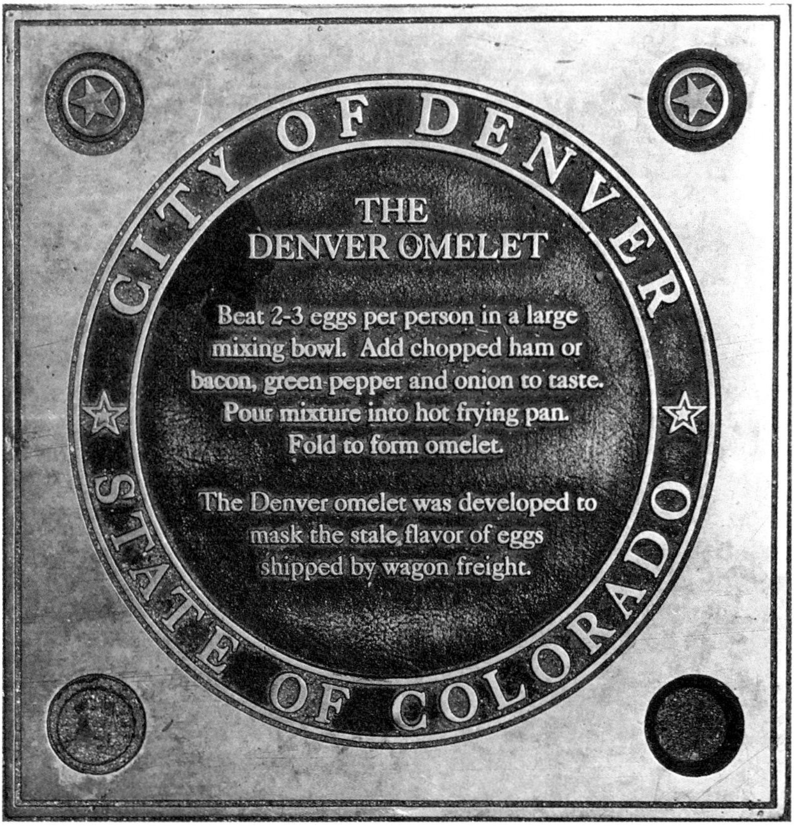

One of a dozen "All Things Colorado" plaques near the 16th & California light rail station, this marker features a recipe and some history, although both angles have skeptics and critics. Photo courtesy of Creative Commons, Brian Rosmaita. https://commons.m.wikimedia.org/wiki/File:Denver-omelet-sidewalk-marker.jpg

Others think it was an adaptation of egg foo yong devised by Chinese railroad workers.

Regardless, the Denver omelet is perhaps one of the three most famous things named for the city, along with the Denver boot and John Denver (born Henry John Deutschendorf Jr.).

A SUNDIAL RISES FROM THE RUBBLE

Where does an oversized, sun-powered timepiece double as playground equipment?

The popular Cranmer Park off of Colorado Boulevard and First Avenue was first established as Mountain View Park in the early 1900s. It owed its original name to a perch in the Hilltop neighborhood with dramatic views of the Rockies to the west, including five peaks that top out at more than 14,000 feet above sea level. At the time, it was the highest point in Denver's city limits.

Longtime Denver Parks and Recreation leader George Cranmer donated an impressive sundial to the park in 1941. Installed on a flagstone terrace, the six-foot disc was inspired by Chinese sundials and crafted from quartzite quarried in Lyons, Colorado, about 20 miles north of Boulder.

The park—later renamed for Cranmer—and the sundial became beloved Hilltop fixtures. The park has been the site of numerous weddings, fireworks viewings, and children "summiting the sundial." Sadly, the original sundial fell victim to vandals who dynamited it to rubble in 1965, and a community-wide effort resulted in the installation of a replica during the subsequent year.

Sundial donor and park namesake George Cranmer is remembered as one of the visionaries behind Red Rocks Park and Amphitheatre in Morrison and the ski area in Winter Park.

The iconic quartzite sundial in Cranmer Park is six feet in diameter, making it the perfect size for a kid to climb. It's actually the second sundial installed in the park; the first was dynamited to smithereens in the 1960s. Photo courtesy of Creative Commons, Gnarlodious. https://commons.wikimedia.org/wiki/File:Cranmer_Sundial.jpg

CRANMER PARK SUNDIAL

What: The second coming of a beloved solar clock

Where: 4501 East 1st Ave.

Cost: Free

Pro Tip: Bring a camera; this is one of the best viewpoints in the city.

A restoration project kicked off in 2013 to restore the sundial and terrace. After organizers raised about $2 million, the project replaced the terrace, added a new mosaic of the mountain panorama, and re-engraved chipped numbers on the sundial's face.

BEFORE BUSES: DENVER'S LOST TROLLEYS

What happened to one of the best urban rail systems in the West?

Denver once had one of the best streetcar, or trolley, systems in the United States, encompassing more than 150 miles of tracks and 250 trolleys, as well as high-speed spurs to Golden and Boulder.

The Denver Tramway Corporation's first streetcars began operating in the city in 1886. In the late 1800s and early 1900s, the city's residents used trolleys (first horse-powered, then electric) to commute to work, get groceries, and visit the amusement parks that were often built at the endpoint of the various lines. In 1917, riders took more than 60 million trips on the system.

However, the golden age of the trolleys didn't last forever. The arrival of the automobile and municipal buses doomed the city's trolleys, and the system shut down once and for all in 1950. Many of the tracks were simply buried in asphalt and forgotten. The advent of light rail in Denver in the 1990s cast doubt on the wisdom of the decision to shut down the system, especially considering the fact that several of the new light rail

---

The original city charter set fares at a nickel in the 1880s. An increase of two cents in 1917 was met with uproar from riders and politicians alike.

This 1895 photograph depicts a streetcar bound for Manhattan Beach, a long-gone amusement park at Sloans Lake. The sign, "Take this car for the Healer," is believed to refer to Francis Schlatter, the "Denver Messiah" (see p. 82). Photo courtesy of the Library of Congress. http://loc.gov/pictures/resource/cph.3c05405/

lines follow the same routes that the trolleys did in their heyday.

The Denver Trolley (formerly known as the Platte Valley Trolley) carries on the tradition today with historic, open-air railcars running a route along the South Platte River just west of downtown every summer.

DENVER'S LOST TROLLEYS

What: The city's original commuter rail system

Where: Citywide (Denver Trolley: 1416 Platte St.)

Cost: Denver Trolley: Adults, $5; children, $2 (children 3 and under, free)

Pro Tip: The Forney Museum of Transportation (4603 Brighton Blvd., Denver) has several historic trolley cars on display.

RED ROCKS: BEHIND THE SCENES

What are the lesser-known tales of the world-class concert venue?

Located 10 miles west of Denver in Morrison, Red Rocks Amphitheatre needs no introduction. The open-air music venue, built into the red sandstone monoliths, has hosted performances by everyone from The Beatles to U2 to Snoop Dogg since opening for concerts in 1906.

The rocks are part of the Fountain Formation, which are thought to have formed nearly 300 million years ago. Ship Rock, Creation Rock, and Stage Rock frame the amphitheatre.

The venue was the brainchild of John Brisben Walker, who lived in a castle above Red Rocks on Mt. Falcon (p. 28). He opened the amphitheatre (then known as Garden of the Titans) in 1906 with a 25-piece brass band and renowned opera star Mary Garden's 1911 concert helped cement its world-class reputation.

After the City of Denver bought Red Rocks for $54,133 in 1927, it got a massive upgrade through the effort of the New Deal–era Civilian Conservation Corps (CCC), and it reopened to the public as a more formal amphitheatre with seating and other amenities in 1941. The workers were honored with a bronze statue in the upper parking lot in 2004, and the old CCC camp below (one of two standing in the country out of 4,500) opened to the public in 2019.

Rock 'n' roll came to Red Rocks in the 1960s with The Beatles (their 1964 concert here was the only non-sellout on their US tour), The Mamas and the Papas, and Jimi Hendrix. In 1971, the rock era was put on pause after a confrontation between unticketed fans and the police during a Jethro Tull

Red Rocks Amphitheatre is one of the most revered concert venues on Earth. In 1999, Pollstar's Best Small Outdoor Concert Venue Award was renamed the Red Rocks Award after the venue won 11 times in a row. Photo courtesy of Red Rocks, www.redrocksonline.com

RED ROCKS AMPHITHEATRE

What: Behind the music, myriad quirks and mysteries

Where: 18300 West Alameda Ave., Morrison

Cost: Free (tickets required for concerts)

Pro Tip: Both the Red Rocks Trading Post (home to the Colorado Music Hall of Fame) and the visitor center (atop the amphitheatre) are well worth a visit.

concert. The ban on rock bands ended in 1976, and Jethro Tull was welcomed back twice in the 2000s.

The amphitheatre is located in Red Rocks Park, with about 10 miles of hiking and biking trails nearby. Below the stage, a secret tunnel leading to the soundboard is plastered with signatures of many musicians who have graced the stage here over the years. Just east of the park, Morrison Cemetery is the source of numerous ghost stories involving hauntings at the amphitheatre and on the surrounding trails.

DAM NO MORE

What was the fate of the dam that was proclaimed unbreakable?

Built across Cherry Creek 40 miles southeast of Denver in 1889–1890, the Castlewood Canyon Dam was touted as an engineering marvel when it was completed, despite the fact that water was visibly seeping through in its early days.

A chunk washed away in 1897, prompting repairs. However, the dam's designers and its owner, the Denver Water Storage Company, pushed back against the public outcry that it was unsafe.

Chief Engineer A. M. Welles responded in a letter at the time, "The Castlewood dam will never, in the life of any person now living, or in generations to come, break to any extent that will do any great damage either to itself or others from the volume of water impounded, and never in all time to the city of Denver."

Fast-forward to August 3, 1933, and Welles was proven wrong when a torrential thunderstorm indeed broke the dam in a big way. The flood hurtled toward Denver in the early morning hours, and a 15-foot wave struck downtown at 7 a.m., leading to two fatalities and millions of dollars of damage in today's dollars.

The dam was never rebuilt; the Cherry Creek Dam has provided flood control closer to Denver since its completion

---

According to a *Time* magazine story, the 1933 flood inundated central Denver with three feet of water, as the jail, police station, and auditorium flooded. Under six inches of water, Union Station saw logs float into the waiting room.

Like the trunkless legs in Percy Bysshe Shelley's "Ozymandias," the Castlewood dam ruins remind us of the folly of bold pronouncements. As Shelley wrote of the crumbling statue, "And on the pedestal, these words appear: 'My name is Ozymandias, King of Kings; Look on my Works, ye Mighty, and despair!'" Photo courtesy of Creative Commons, Eric Lumsden. https://www.flickr.com/photos/64604717@N03/9228312940

CASTLEWOOD CANYON DAM

What: The unbreakable dam sits in ruins.

Where: Castlewood Canyon State Park, 2989 Colorado Hwy. 83, Franktown

Cost: $9 per vehicle

Pro Tip: The 0.35-mile Dam Trail accesses the ruins.

in 1950. The ruins of the Castlewood Canyon Dam remain in place as a memorial to the 1933 flood at Castlewood Canyon State Park.

I. M. PEI'S LIVING CITY

How did the iconic architect hone his craft in the Mile High City?

Ieoh Ming Pei, better known by his initials, is the Chinese American architect who rose to the top of his field before his passing at age 102 in 2019.

Before winning accolades and awards for such projects as the National Gallery East in Washington, D.C., the Louvre Pyramid in Paris, and the Rock and Roll Hall of Fame in Cleveland, Pei cut his teeth on a series of projects in Denver in the 1950s.

At 17th and Broadway, the Mile High Center featured a sleek tower and a plaza with a waterfall running alongside a staircase into a stocked trout pond. Also known as Zeckendorf Plaza, Courthouse Square featured a distinctive parabolic pavilion that housed an ice rink.

In *Conversations with I. M. Pei: Light is the Key*, by Gero Von Boehm, Pei was quoted on his experience in Denver: "I learned the process of development, and about the city as a living organism."

I. M. PEI IN DENVER

What: The architectural legend's work in Denver launched his career.

Where: Multiple locations

Cost: Free

Pro Tip: The National Center for Atmospheric Research in Boulder offers free tours.

Pei's standout structure in Colorado is still standing in Boulder: The National Center for Atmospheric Research, built in the 1960s, took cues from Buddhist temples, Ancestral Puebloan cliff dwellings, and cubist design.

Now the Sheraton Denver Hotel, this tower was one of I. M. Pei's early designs in Denver. It opened as the Denver Hilton at Zeckendorf Plaza, a.k.a. Courthouse Square, in the heart of downtown. Photo courtesy of Creative Commons, Eric A. Schiff. https://commons.wikimedia.org/wiki/File:DenverSheraton-Tower-15.JPG

The best-known Pei design in Denver is the 16th Street Mall, This pedestrian street in the heart of downtown came in the 1980s, but most of Pei's contributions to Denver's urban fabric were wiped out by redevelopment. While the 16th Street Mall remains, the plaza at Mile High Center was replaced in 1980 by an atrium that was a nod to the famed "cash register building" a block away, and the pavilion at courthouse square was demolished to make way for a hotel in the 1990s.

AN IGLOO, RATTLESNAKES, AND FDR

Where is the largest collection of New Deal–supported buildings in Colorado?

The Colorado National Guard established the State Rifle Range three miles east of Golden in 1903. As the only permanent training facility of the Colorado National Guard, it was the site of summer encampments, and its role expanded as a hub for the Works Progress Administration in Colorado during the Great Depression.

Dubbed Camp George West (after Golden newspaper publisher George West) in 1934, the site saw significant development in the years that followed. An open-air amphitheater on the southern flank of South Table Mountain, Colorado Amphitheater was completed in 1935. Its 2,500 seats make it the second-largest historic open-air amphitheater in the state, bested in size only

CAMP GEORGE WEST

What: A history book at the base of South Table Mountain

Where: 15000 South Golden Rd., Golden

Cost: Free

Pro Tip: Bring boots to hike the trails at adjacent South Table Mountain Park if you visit. There is a trailhead at Camp George West.

During the peak of the Works Progress Administration in the 1930s, Camp George West had 29 mess halls. Nine of them serve as a correctional facility today.

Along with historic buildings from the early 1900s and World War II–era military facilities, Camp George West is home to the largest collection of surviving Works Progress Administration structures in Colorado. Photo courtesy of Creative Commons, Hustvedt. https://commons.wikimedia.org/wiki/File:Camp_George_West_Golden_CO.jpg

by Red Rocks (see p. 74) in Morrison. It was used to screen films for the guardsmen but was later abandoned due to the prevalence of rattlesnakes. It's now owned by the nearby National Renewable Energy Laboratory.

Amid numerous Craftsman-style bungalows, Building 45, the historic headquarters, and Ammunition Igloo, built in 1940 from locally quarried basalt and an earthen roof, are two notable surviving structures.

Listed on the National Register of Historic Places as the Camp George Historic District in 1993, the 98-acre site is now home to several state agencies alongside facilities still in use by the Colorado National Guard.

DENVER'S VANISHING MESSIAH

Was Francis Schlatter a humble cobbler or a divine healer?

Francis Schlatter was a cobbler. For a while, he repaired shoes and boots. Later, he repaired bodies and souls.

Schlatter, variously nicknamed "The Vanishing Messiah," "the Denver Messiah," and "the Great Healer," appeared one day in North Denver and began healing people—an estimated 60,000 in all.

Born in a village in Alsace, France, in 1856, Schlatter immigrated to the United States and worked his trade in various cities until 1892, when he arrived in Denver.

Soon after, Schlatter heard what he said was the voice of "the Father" commanding him to heal the sick. The voice also ordered him to lift weights and walk 10 miles a day.

Schlatter already was plenty strong; people said they witnessed him twisting horseshoes with his bare hands

He began a two-year walk around the South and Midwest, interrupted only when he was jailed in Arkansas for vagrancy. He quickly escaped and resumed his travels.

He said he had nothing to teach, but was obeying the wishes of the Father. Asked if he was the Christ, he simply said, "Yes."

EDWARD L. FOX HOUSE

What: Francis Schlatter healed thousands from the home of Denver councilman Edward L. Fox.

Where: 3225 Quivas St.

Cost: Free to view, not open to the public

Pro Tip: For more, see a handful of biographies or the Denver Public Library Western History Collection, Denver Central Library, 10 West 14th Ave. Pkwy.

With his penetrating eyes and long hair, Francis Schlatter bore a resemblance to Jesus Christ, according to some. Schlatter, a French immigrant, began his time in Denver as a humble cobbler and ended it as a mysterious mass healer and mystic. Photo courtesy of Wikimedia Commons

Schlatter briefly settled south of Albuquerque, New Mexico, where his mass healing began at a clip of about 2,000 people per day. One beneficiary of his touch was Denver city councilman Edward Fox, who invited Schlatter to return to Denver with him.

Tens of thousands of people flocked to Fox's North Denver bungalow. After about four months of healing, Schlatter left Fox a note saying his mission was complete, stole a white horse, and disappeared.

Some said he was seen again in New Mexico. Later, a skeleton found in Mexico was said to have been his. A handful of impostors appeared around the country claiming to be Schlatter, but in the end, it appeared the Denver Messiah had vanished into thin air.

Francis Schlatter appeared in Denver, disappeared, then appeared again, healed about 60,000 people, and disappeared again—forever—leaving an eternal mystery behind.

LAMB SPRING'S PREHISTORIC SECRETS

What prehistoric hunting site south of Denver yielded record numbers of mammoth remains?

Lamb Spring isn't even a spring, its waters having died a natural death in 1970. Today the site appears to be a nondescript patch of rolling prairie a couple of miles east of the foothills of the Rocky Mountains.

Yet the 35-acre Lamb Spring Archaeological Preserve is an important prehistoric site where scientists have found evidence indicating that Paleo-humans lived and hunted in North America more than 8,000 years ago.

In ancient days, the spring was a favorite watering hole for ancient American horses, ground sloths, camels, bison, and Columbian mammoths, great beasts standing about 13 feet high and weighing as much as 11 tons.

That's why Lamb Spring was a popular place for human hunters, who used spears to kill bison—and possibly other animals—that had gathered to drink.

Lamb Spring's oldest layer yielded the world's largest collection of Columbian mammoth remains—perhaps 33 of the great beasts.

Radiocarbon dating shows mammoth bones at Lamb Spring from a period of about 500 years, some nearly 12,000 years

LAMB SPRING ARCHAEOLOGICAL PRESERVE

What: Paleo-humans hunted prehistoric beasts here 8,000 years ago.

Where: Near the intersection of West Titan Road and North Rampart Range Road, Roxborough Park

Cost: Free, but you must register for a tour

Pro Tip: Go to www.lambspring.org to arrange for a free lecture tour.

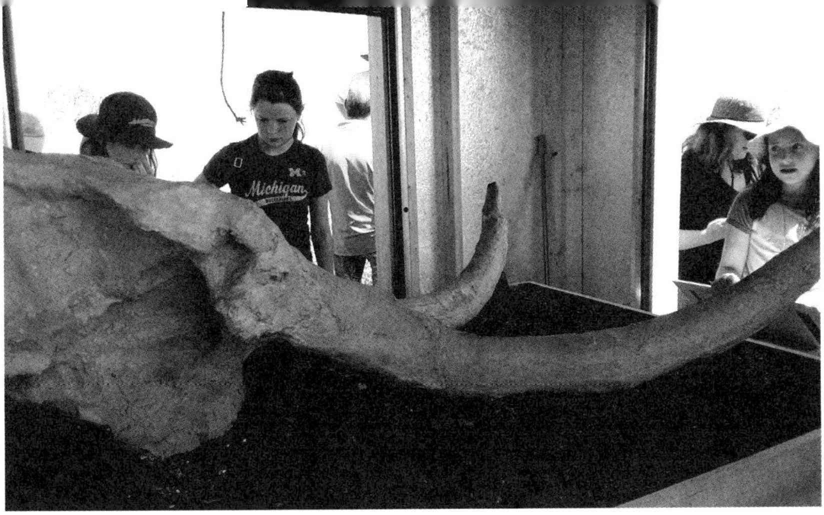

Lamb Spring Archaeological Preserve contained the remains of more than 30 Columbian mammoths, the largest number ever discovered in one place. Here, tourists observe a reproduction of a female mammoth skull found on the site. The original is now at the Denver Museum of Nature & Science. Photo courtesy of David B. Lewis

old. It appears those ancient mammoths died of natural causes and might have been scavenged by humans in the neighborhood.

Scientists are doubtful, but some are intrigued by mammoth bones there with what could be butcher marks, along with a great stone that might have been used as an ancient butcher block.

The dig at the site also uncovered a higher layer of Cody Culture-era bison hunters about 8,000 years old, including several stone knives and scrapers.

The excavation since has been filled in, awaiting further funding. All that's visible now is a metal hut containing reproductions of ancient knives and tools and a copy of a skull of a young female mammoth. The original was discovered at Lamb Spring's low point, precisely where the hut is located.

Sixty years ago, Charles Lamb discovered a natural spring on his land about 20 miles south of downtown Denver. Lamb soon discovered bones there—including a mammoth tusk.

THE BAFFLING DISAPPEARANCE OF PROF. THOMAS RIHA

One day in 1969, a distinguished University of Colorado professor vanished without a trace. Who was the real Thomas Riha?

About 50 years ago, Prof. Thomas Riha vanished.

In 1967, Riha joined the faculty of the University of Colorado Boulder at the age of 40. He was a renowned Russia scholar and editor of the prestigious three-volume *Readings in Russian Civilization*, just one of his books that remains in print to this day.

On March 20, 1969, Riha failed to show up for his college classes. Boulder police went to his home, where they found his kitchen table set for breakfast and his clothes and toiletries laid out but untouched.

A woman named Galya Tannenbaum said she had contacted Riha in Montreal, and that she was authorized to dispose of his home and other property.

Tannenbaum is central to this strange tale. Riha believed she was a colonel in Army Intelligence. She evidently had attempted to gas Riha's wife. A few months after the professor's disappearance, two of her friends died of cyanide poisoning,

---

Prof. Thomas Riha, a Czech immigrant, was an expert in Russian history and language. One day he suddenly disappeared forever, leaving a datebook that included the puzzling notation, "Dinner Colonel."

When Prof. Thomas Riha disappeared, all sorts of wild rumors sprang to life. Riha was a CIA agent. No—he was a Soviet spy. The Boulder Police Department said he had left voluntarily and that "an agency" had said not to be concerned. The FBI declined comment. Photo courtesy of Denver Public Library

leaving wills behind naming her their beneficiary.

The authorities investigated, and the Boulder district attorney charged Tannenbaum with a couple of counts of forgery. Later, a search of her home uncovered Riha's passport and driver's license, and a pound of potassium cyanide in her basement.

Tannenbaum pleaded not guilty of forgery by reason of insanity and was committed to the State Hospital in Pueblo. There, in 1971, Tannenbaum committed suicide by ingestion of . . . potassium cyanide.

Her last words: "Of everything I've done, I didn't kill Riha."

Riha's disappearance continued to produce ripples, including a rift between the CIA and FBI. The CIA went to lengths to avoid answering questions about him, including inquiries from the Denver district attorney, the US Senate Intelligence Committee, and a federal judge.

Riha was declared legally dead in 1978, and his estate was wound up the following year. No trace of him was ever found.

THOMAS RIHA'S NEIGHBORHOOD

What: Thomas Riha was a University of Colorado professor and Russia expert who one day vanished into thin air.

Where: Riha's former home is located at 6th and College Avenues in Boulder.

Cost: Free, not open to the public

Pro Tip: For more information, see the Denver Public Library's Western History and Genealogy Department's biography clippings of Thomas Riha and Galya Tannenbaum, Denver Central Library, 10 W. 14th Ave. Pkwy.

ROCKY MOUNTAIN ARSENAL NATIONAL WILDLIFE REFUGE (page 2)

Photo courtesy of USFWS

UNION STATION (page 156)
Photo by Eric Peterson

FROZEN DEAD GUY DAYS (page 168)
Photo courtesy of Flickr, Daniel Oberhaus

RUDY PROJECT
HARLEM
HARLEM

WEST BIJOU RANCH (page 24)
Photo courtesy of Byron Shelton, Savory Institute

COLORADO STATE CAPITOL (page 148)
Photo courtesy of Wikipedia Commons, Daderot

CAMP GEORGE WEST (page 80)
Photo courtesy of Wikimedia Commons, Jeffrey Beall

DENVER BOTANIC GARDENS (page 146)

Photo by Eric Peterson

LAKESIDE AMUSEMENT PARK (page 38)
Photo by Eric Peterson

DENVER INTERNATIONAL AIRPORT (page 122)
Photo courtesy of Wikimedia Commons, David Benbennick

RED ROCKS AMPHITHEATRE (page 74)
Photo by Eric Peterson

CITY OF KUNMING PARK (page 32)
Photo by Eric Peterson

WWW.PC

BARNUM IN DENVER (page 8)
Photo by Eric Peterson

BOULDER ATOMIC CLOCK (page 150)
Photo courtesy of Wikimedia Commons, NIST

BROWN PALACE (page 136)
Photo by Eric Peterson

COLORADO'S SECOND-GREATEST DIAMOND SWINDLE

Were Antonio Ciccarelli and Nicholas John Digiallonardo diamond swindlers, or were they simply following a longtime Colorado tradition?

The Great Diamond Swindle it was not, but in 1967, a couple of Denverites came close to duplicating the more famous fraud right here in the Mile High City.

The actual Great Diamond Swindle was perpetrated in the 1870s by a couple of con men who sprinkled diamonds on a field in a remote corner of the then-Colorado Territory. The hoax was much admired for its roster of world-renowned suckers, including Horace Greeley, Charles Tiffany, and Baron von Rothschild.

The 1967 Pretty Great Diamond Swindle lacked the well-heeled patronage of its predecessor.

Antonio Ciccarelli and Nicholas John Digiallonardo were con artists who conceived of a simple swindle: They would inform their patsy that they had a cache of diamonds for sale at a steep discount, then switch real diamonds for fakes.

The con artists' undoing came when they met a traveling salesman named Kaylor Glasgow. Glasgow had a side gig, buying diamonds on the road and selling them at a profit back in Colorado. A confederate introduced Glasgow to Digiallonardo

Traveling salesman Kaylor Glasgow was introduced to swindlers Antonio Ciccarelli and Nicholas John Digiallonardo, who made him an offer he couldn't refuse—until he did.

Antonio Ciccarelli and Nicholas John Digiallonardo sought success through a simple diamond bait-and-switch scam. Their hoax served them well until a salesman named Kaylor Glasgow tipped off the Denver cops and the FBI. Photo courtesy of Denver Public Library

and Ciccarelli, who offered diamonds worth $100,000 for just $12,000.

Glasgow insisted on taking the gems to an expert. The con men declined, but after much back-and-forth, they agreed to part with the diamonds for only $7,500, promising a refund if Glasgow wasn't satisfied. Glasgow paid, had the diamonds appraised, found out they were phonies, and then returned for a refund.

Ciccarelli and Digiallonardo were gone.

The con depended on the dubious bona fides of their marks, who, being crooks themselves, would be reluctant to involve the police.

Not Glasgow—he complained to the cops. Digiallonardo and Ciccarelli in short order were arrested by the FBI and ultimately convicted of running a confidence game and conspiracy. Sentenced to one to five years in prison, they were never heard from again.

DIAMOND PEAK

What: Colorado has hosted two notable diamond swindles, one that gave its name to Diamond Peak in northwest Colorado.

Where: The Great Diamond Swindle salted its diamonds around Diamond Peak, in northwest Colorado's Moffat County.

Cost: Free

Pro Tip: For more on Ciccarelli and Digiallonardo, the best source is the Denver Public Library's Western History and Genealogy Department's clippings files, Denver Central Library, 10 W. 14th Ave. Pkwy.

COLORADO CHAUTAUQUA BRINGS BACK THE GOOD OL' DAYS

Where can you find the only year-round chautauqua in the United States?

In their heyday, hundreds of chautauquas dotted the United States. Now just a handful remain.

The chautauqua movement started in 1874 in its namesake town in New York State. The idea was to combine vacations and day visits with adult education and entertainment.

The notion caught fire, and chautauquas were built all around the country. The movement peaked in the early 1920s, but declined with the growing popularity of movies and radio.

The only remaining year-round chautauqua is Boulder's beautiful Colorado Chautauqua, nestled in Chautauqua Park in the shadow of Green Mountain and the famous Boulder Flatirons.

Today, the Colorado Chautauqua is a National Historic Landmark and the only chautauqua west of the Mississippi River to have operated continuously since its founding.

The Colorado Chautauqua also is the only Western chautauqua with all its original buildings intact, including the renowned Chautauqua Dining Hall.

The Colorado Chautauqua is the centerpiece of beautiful Chautauqua Park, which features a picnic area, playground, demonstration garden, and hiking trails to Green Mountain and the Boulder Flatirons.

Unchanged since 1898, the Colorado Chautauqua's entertainment today ranges from summertime's Colorado Music Festival to Meadow Music programs, a combination of music and nature education. It also rents homes from small cottages to Missions House Lodge, a 3,197-square-foot, eight-bedroom lodge with full kitchen. Photo courtesy of Wikimedia Commons

THE COLORADO CHAUTAUQUA

What: The Colorado Chautauqua is the only remaining year-round chautauqua, the only one with all its original buildings intact, and the only one with hiking trails to the Colorado Rockies.

Where: 900 Baseline Rd., Boulder

Cost: Free to visit; other costs depend on the price of entertainment and amenities.

Pro Tip: Bring your hiking boots and an appetite—the Chautauqua Dining Hall serves brunch and dinner and, in summer, it operates a beer garden.

Chautauqua entertainment might consist of a speech by fiery preacher Billy Sunday or lecturer Russell Conwell, who delivered his "Acres of Diamonds" speech about 6,000 times.

Chautauquas featured speakers, preachers, teachers and musicians, not to mention monologists, elocutionists, jugglers, magicians, whistlers, and yodelers.

The Colorado Chautauqua started when the Texas Board of Regents decided to offer a summer school for teachers in a cool, inviting setting. More than 4,000 people crowded opening day, July 4, 1898.

Today's Colorado Chautauqua is not all that much different from that of the olden days, a plain wooden structure hosting lectures on such topics as space exploration, paranormal research, nature appreciation, and children's books; music from Mozart to the blues; plus a silent movie series and the Boulder Concert Band.

DENVER'S COLD WAR TIME MACHINE

Ever wished you could travel back to the bad ol' days of the Cold War?

The Federal Emergency Management Agency (FEMA) has something special going on at its Denver regional headquarters: a journey back in time.

That's because its Region VIII headquarters is two sites in one. The building acts both as a working office for Rocky Mountain region emergencies and a model Cold War fortress.

The headquarters' main building was constructed in 1969, when nuclear fear and paranoia ruled the day and guided the FEMA building's design. That's why the complex is constructed on two levels; the upper level is under three feet of earth, and the lower one is entirely belowground.

The FEMA headquarters was made mainly of steel, for strength, and concrete, to protect occupants from gamma rays. It was constructed to withstand the worst conceivable nuclear attack, with main and back-up generators, a 5,000-gallon water tank supplemented by an 800-foot-deep well, and air intake designed to filter out radioactive particles.

On the north side of the lobby, steel vault blast doors lead to an underground bunker. At one time, this underground portion of building 710 included male and female dormitories, medical facilities, a kitchen and lunchroom, and, most impressively, a

---

FEMA's Rocky Mountain region headquarters remains close to its original concept: a shelter from nuclear war designed to shield a staff of 300 for a month.

The photo above was taken in 1973, four years after construction of FEMA's Rocky Mountain region complex. Originally, it included dormitories, a kitchen and cafeteria, and amenities such as a "metal box room" to protect communications equipment from an electromagnetic pulse. Photo courtesy of FEMA

FEMA IN DENVER

What: FEMA's Region VIII regional headquarters was a bunker designed to withstand a nuclear attack.

Where: Denver Federal Center, Building 710

Cost: Free

Pro Tip: Visitors can observe the building exterior in the Denver Federal Center, but public tours are not available due to the building's strict security.

giant coffee urn built right into the plumbing.

Many of these features are gone now, alas, and 710's bunker now consists mostly of windowless offices, albeit with ultra-fancy communications equipment.

Another set of doors leads from the lobby through a long hallway illuminated on either side by lights embedded in the floor, rather like the lights that run along the sides of a jet plane's corridor. These lead to building 710A, which today is an almost normal-seeming office space—for an underground emergency management agency, that is.

HISTORIC ELITCH THEATRE TO RISE AGAIN . . . AND AGAIN

The Elitch Theatre was a jewel of the American stage until it suffered a series of reverses. Does it have one more comeback left?

For more than a century, Denver's Historic Elitch Theatre was one of the brightest stars in the galaxy of America's stage showcases. Now the great stage is empty, the victim of time and devastating setbacks.

The Historic Elitch Theatre was built in 1891 as the centerpiece of Elitch Gardens, an amusement park and home of the first major zoo west of Chicago.

Elitch Theatre launched America's first summer stock company and exhibited Colorado's first movies. It ceased theater operations in 1991.

In 1994, Elitch Gardens moved to central Denver, leaving a couple of buildings behind, including the theater.

Many of America's greatest performers trod the Elitch boards. The 1905 season alone featured Tyrone Power Sr.; director Cecil B. DeMille; Antoinette Perry, actress, director, and namesake of Broadway's Tony Awards; and Denver East High School graduate Douglas Fairbanks, a lifetime achievement Oscar winner. Fairbanks got his start at the Elitch Theatre,

---

Denver's Historic Elitch Theatre reigned as an outstanding summer stock showplace, featuring stars such as Grace Kelly, Myrna Loy, Walter Pidgeon, Edward G. Robinson, Debbie Reynolds, and Ginger Rogers.

The Historic Elitch Theatre remains much as it was when the structure was completed in 1891. Exterior renovations were complete when, in 2018, a hailstorm crashed the building's flagpole into its roof and wrenched apart its awning, causing an estimated $1 million in damage. Photo courtesy of Wikimedia Commons

sweeping the stage for tickets. Douglas Fairbanks Jr. also performed at the Elitch Theatre, from 1971 to 1973.

Still-active actors who performed there include Robert Redford, Bernadette Peters, Cloris Leachman, and William Shatner.

Fundraising efforts for the theater began before its official closing. In the early 1990s, actor and alumnus Raymond Burr (*Perry Mason*) raised $2 million for an education program there. The money instead was donated to a local middle school.

In 2002, the Historic Elitch Gardens Theatre Foundation began raising money to restore and maintain the theater and the carousel pavilion next door. Renovations began a few years later. Much of the restoration was completed in 2014.

Then disaster struck in 2018 when a hailstorm caused about $1 million in damage to the theater's roof and awning. Volunteers continue to raise funds to repair the historic structure. They swear the show will go on, someday.

THE HISTORIC ELITCH THEATRE

What: Denver's Historic Elitch Theatre awaits a chance to reclaim its former theatrical glory.

Where: 4655 West 37th Pl.

Cost: Free

Pro Tip: The Historic Elitch Theatre is closed, but it remains the centerpiece of a mini-complex that includes the theater, the Theatre Plaza, and the Carousel Pavilion—ideal for picnics!

A PRISTINE TRIP BACK TO GOLD BOOM TIMES

Where can you find old-time Colorado, untouched since the gold boom?

Forty-some miles northwest of Denver, 20-some miles west of Boulder, lies a too-often-overlooked invitation to Colorado's past.

The Eldora Historic District offers visitors a living, breathing glimpse of old-time Colorado.

Eldora today boasts a population of fewer than 200 souls and a whole lot of scenery ranging from an altitude of 8,600 feet to more than 11,000 feet above sea level.

The town lies within a valley bisected by Middle Boulder Creek, nine miles from the Continental Divide. Encompassed by the Roosevelt National Forest, Eldora lies downhill from Eldora Mountain Resort, a ski area comprising 26 miles of ski runs.

The heart of Eldora is its historic district, consisting of 30 acres and 67 log and rustic buildings constructed at the end of the 19th century and the beginning of the 20th century.

Back then, Eldora was a mining town in the middle of a short-lived gold boom. At its height, Eldora had a population of about 1,300.

Today, most of the buildings in the district are small log dwellings unchanged since the boom days, constructed without plumbing, foundations, or ornaments.

At the heart of the Eldora Historic District is the Goldminer Hotel, built in 1897. Originally a two-story log building, the

---

Near the Eldora Mountain Resort ski area, the Eldora Historic District displays a mountain mining community untouched by time.

Eldora Historic District, an easy day trip from Denver, preserves mountain life the way it was from the 1870s through the early 20th century. Dozens of original homes and businesses dot its 30 acres. Photo courtesy of Wikimedia Commons

ELDORA HISTORIC DISTRICT

What: A great day trip in combination with Eldora Mountain Resort

Where: A half-mile from the Nederland traffic circle, turn right on Eldorado Avenue and drive 3.3 miles. The Goldminer Hotel is located at 601 Klondyke Ave.

Cost: Free

Pro Tip: The historic Goldminer Hotel accommodates 12 guests and offers a lobby, a kitchen, five bedrooms, four baths, and a "social room" added in 1934. Call 303-258-7770 or 800-422-4629 for reservations.

structure was fancified by a clapboard façade supported by four decorative columns. The log building remains clearly visible on three sides.

In 1897, a critical year for Eldora, the town government was organized and the settlement was awarded a post office. Back then, Eldora was called Eldorado Camp, until the postal authorities insisted it be renamed Eldora to avoid confusion with the California mining camp of the same name.

DENVER'S SHOCKING COLD CASE

Will we ever know who killed four United Bank security guards and stole almost $200,000?

At 9:14 a.m. on Father's Day, June 16, 1991, a man began murdering his way through the then-United Bank Tower in downtown Denver. When he was finished, the bank was missing almost $200,000, four security guards had been slain, and Denver was left with the most shocking unsolved case in its history.

The Father's Day Bank Massacre began when a man calling himself a vice president used a telephone outside the bank to ask security guards for entry through a freight elevator. When guard William McCullum Jr. opened the elevator doors, the man shot him dead and hid his body in the bank's subbasement.

The assailant then took McCullum's pass card and negotiated tunnels up one story to the guard room. There, he forced guards Scott McCarthy and Phillip Mankoff into a side room and killed them. Guard Todd Wilson entered the area. The killer slew him, too, and took videotapes and other potential evidence.

The killer then entered the bank vault area, where he imprisoned six employees in a "mantrap," a room adjacent to the vault. He took more than $197,000 and escaped 42 minutes after entering the bank.

He had removed all the shell casings used in his shootings, leaving behind only the bullets he had fired.

Both the prosecution and the defense of James King had solid-sounding arguments. But after 53 hours of jury deliberation, he was set free.

Four bank guards were murdered in the United Bank Tower (today called the Wells Fargo Center) in what became known as the Father's Day Bank Massacre. One key point in favor of the accused, James King: the unreliability of eyewitnesses, who were baffled by a photo of a man disguised like the perpetrator. It turned out to be actor Harrison Ford. Photo courtesy of Wikipedia Commons, Onetwo1, https://commons.wikimedia.org/wiki/File:Wellsfargocenterdenver1.JPG

More than 60 local police officers and FBI agents began investigating. Less than three weeks later, on July 4, they arrested former Denver police officer and former part-time United Bank security guard James King.

King's trial began the next May. Three weeks later, the jury found King not guilty.

An alternative suspect, another former bank security guard, intrigued investigators but was never charged.

The shadow of the Father's Day Bank Massacre hung over King the rest of his life. He died in 2013.

UNITED BANK CENTER

What: The Father's Day Bank Massacre and its aftermath riveted Denver for years.

Where: The former United Bank Center, now the Wells Fargo Center, 1700 Lincoln St.

Cost: Free

Pro Tip: If you can find it, read 1997's *Murders in the Bank Vault: The Father's Day Massacre and the Trial of James King*, by King's legendary defense attorney Walter Gerash and Denver historian Phil Goodstein.

SHHH . . . SPOOKY SECRETS OF DENVER'S LUMBER BARON INN

What are the secrets of Denver's mystery mansion?

Today, Denver's Lumber Baron Inn & Gardens is a successful bed and breakfast.

The inn receives rave reviews for its delicious dishes, weekend brunches, wine dinners, sumptuous wedding ceremonies, and special events such as "Death Café," "Poe in the Parlor," and "Witches Tea." Ah, but there's so much more to the Lumber Baron Inn, so much that could be called eerie, creepy, and macabre.

Even in a notoriously spook-ridden city like Denver, the Lumber Baron Inn long has stood out as a locus for the supernatural, the ghostly, and the ghastly.

Before it became the Lumber Baron Inn, the place was known as the John Mouat Mansion, after the (what else) lumber baron who built the 8,500-square-foot, Queen Anne–style mansion in 1890.

Alas, Mouat, broken by the Panic of 1893, signed the mansion over to his bank.

Time was unkind to the inn. It hit bottom in 1970 with the killings of Kara Lee Knoche, 17, and Marianne Weaver, 18. Their murders were never solved.

In 1991, Walter Keller bought the mansion for $80,000, renovated it, and ran it until 2016, when he sold it for $1.7 million to Joel and Elaine Bryant.

The Lumber Baron Inn & Gardens is a popular, flourishing bed and breakfast with a long and storied history of ghostly goings-on.

Denver's Lumber Baron Inn & Gardens is a gorgeous example of Queen Anne Revival–style architecture and a great spot for afternoon tea, breakfast brunch, indoor and outdoor weddings—or some serious ghost hunting. Photo courtesy of The Lumber Baron Inn & Gardens

THE LUMBER BARON INN & GARDENS

What: The Lumber Baron Inn has a famous history of mysterious phenomena and great breakfast buffets.

Where: 2555 West 37th Ave.

Cost: Rooms start at $169 per night to the $259 per night Honeymoon Suite.

Pro Tip: See the inn's garden for a perfect site for weddings and other special events.

Keller often heard eerie sounds and felt strange cold breezes. Once, working outside the room where Knoche and Weaver had been killed, he felt a presence over his shoulder and a frigid wind.

Nor are the spirits of the two the only supernatural presences detected in the inn, which include a scolding schoolteacher, a cigarette-smoking flapper, a mother of the bride, an undulating staircase, strange reflections in old mirrors, and the frequent feeling that guests are being watched by the unseen—not to mention cold spots, cold breaths, and rising goosebumps.

Have fun!

THE 5 STAR SALT CAVES SECRET

How did a salt cave get built less than three miles south of downtown Denver?

Denver's 5 Star Salt Caves is just your typical salt cave—if you consider "typical" a cave made of 13,000 pounds of Himalayan rock salt less than three miles from downtown Denver—with a secret, to boot.

In case you've been living in another kind of cave, salt caves and related salty facilities have become quite the thing. There are about 100 caves nationwide, more than 600 salt therapy sites, and an industry group, the Boca Raton, Florida–based Salt Therapy Association.

But Denver's 5 Star Salt Caves establishment has elements that make it special, as well as a secret we'll get to in a moment.

The cave itself is made mostly of pink salt mined from Pakistani caves. The salt contains 84 minerals said to mirror the mineral content of the human body. Pink salt fills the floor of the cave, and bricks of salt line its walls. Illumination is provided by tiny LED lights and a dozen salt bricks lit from behind. The cave also features a ventilation system that blows micro-quantities of salt into the air.

The idea of dry salt therapy, known as halotherapy, is that exposure to dry salt and its mineral content clears the lungs and sinuses, has overall good physical effects, and feels pretty peaceful too.

The United States hosts about 100 human-made therapeutic salt caves, but Denver's has a secret.

It takes a lot of salt to make a salt cave—about 13,000 pounds worth in this case—and a lot of know-how. In the case of Denver's salt cave, the salt portions consist of a salt floor, a salt brick wall, and a salt-blowing ventilation system. Photo courtesy of 5 Star Salt Caves

5 STAR SALT CAVES

What: Denver's 5 Star Salt Caves has a 400-square-foot salt cave and lots of other therapeutic facilities. How the cave was built remains hush-hush.

Where: 722 South Pearl St.

Cost: Prices range from $35 for a 50-minute salt cave session for an adult ($10 for a child) to packages including the cave and other services for up to $115.

Pro Tip: In case your salt cave neighbors are noisy, management supplies ear plugs. But you might prefer bringing your own earbuds or headphones.

The business also features a massage room, an infrared sauna, a room for an ionic footbath built into the plumbing, and other features, including a therapy room, store, and meeting room.

So what's the secret?

Ask yourself a question: How would one stick those salt bricks together to make salt walls? You can't use concrete because salt would crack it apart. You can't use glue, because who wants to sit in a salt cave inhaling glue?

How do you put it together?

That's the secret.

RIDDLES OF DENVER INTERNATIONAL AIRPORT

Why is Denver International Airport a magnet for rumors and conspiracy theories and home to its very own 9,000-pound demon horse?

From its beginning, Denver International Airport (DIA) has been plagued by a strange combination of construction snafus and bizarre conspiracy theories.

The apparent curse bedeviling DIA is best symbolized by the *Blue Mustang*, the 32-foot-high sculpture that greets drivers approaching the airport. The blue fiberglass horse is popularly known as the demon horse—a.k.a. Blucifer—thanks to its blue coat and glowing red eyes. Also creepy is the fact that in 2006, part of it fell and killed its sculptor, Luis Jiménez.

Perhaps the airport was born under a bad sign. The opening of DIA (as it is known locally) or DEN (as it is known to the aviation world) was delayed for 16 months, and it ran $2 billion over budget. This was mainly due to an experimental, high-tech baggage-handling system that tended to eat luggage and toss it in all directions. It took managers 10 years to give up on the disastrous idea.

DENVER INTERNATIONAL AIRPORT

What: Denver International Airport has had plenty of real-world problems and just as many unreal-world problems.

Where: 8500 Peña Blvd.

Cost: Free to visit, plus parking costs

Pro Tip: With its ongoing—and virtually everlasting—construction problems, it always pays to arrive at least two hours before flight time.

Denver International Airport's entrance is dominated by the Blue Mustang*, also known as Blucifer or the demon horse, a towering red-eyed sculpture that is admired and despised in equal measure. Photo courtesy of Wikimedia Commons*

Yet DIA's checkered past pales next to its rumored reality.

Probably the most prevalent theory regarding DIA's hidden side is the persistent tale that beneath the airport lies a linked series of hidden bunkers and mysterious tunnels. It is indeed true that there are about 470,000 square feet of tunnels under DIA, mostly used for baggage handling.

But how to explain other Denver airport stories? Are its runways really patterned like a swastika? Are its sculptures and decorative murals secret code for an alien invasion? Is its time capsule a message from the Illuminati?

Maybe. Or maybe not.

Denver's airport has been plagued by cost overruns, construction nightmares, and rumors that it is an outpost of the New World Order. Or hidden Nazis. Or outer-space aliens. Or something.

LINGER EATUARY'S DEATHLY SECRETS

What popular Denver restaurant used to be Denver's biggest mortuary?

Linger Eatuary either overcame or built upon its origins as a mortuary to become one of the city's most popular dining spots.

Once Denver's biggest mortuary, the then Olinger Mortuary was long best known for preparing the remains of "Buffalo Bill" Cody in 1917 (see p. 4).

Owner and chef Justin Cucci converted the abandoned mortuary into an "eatuary" by taking the original, humongous Olinger's Mortuary sign, turning off the "O" and changing the sign's "Mort" portion to "Eat."

Apparently, few diners are squeamish about the restaurant's deathly past. In fact, the eatery capitalizes on its origins by offering coffin-shaped menus, drinks in the kinds of bottles that used to contain formaldehyde, and metal coffin conveyors used as dining tables.

The portion of the place just below its iconic sign was named one of "America's Coolest Rooftop Bars" by *Travel+Leisure* magazine, and the restaurant also has received recognition for its hip patio, scrumptious brunches, and "Happenin' Hood."

Less well-known is the link between the mortuary and its one-time owner, Francis Van Derbur.

Once upon a time, Denver's popular Linger Eatuary was a well-known mortuary whose ex-owner's terrible secret was revealed by his daughter, a former Miss America.

For years, the Olinger Mortuary was known far and wide for its towering illuminated sign. With a couple of minor changes the sign served to light the "Linger Eatuary." Photo courtesy of Flickr, Tadson Bussey

Van Derbur owned Olinger's and other Denver-area mortuaries and for years was one of Denver's most celebrated philanthropists and socialites.

The icing on his cake was the fame of his daughter, Marilyn Van Derbur, who was crowned Miss America of 1958.

Then, in 1991, Marilyn Van Derbur said her father had sexually molested her from age 5 to age 18.

Denverites were horrified. Many initially were doubtful. Later, a sister who had been similarly abused confirmed her account.

LINGER EATUARY

What: A popular restaurant and a converted mortuary that has been nationally recognized for its food, its rather strange setting, and its unique rooftop bar.

Where: 2030 West 30th Ave.

Cost: The menu changes regularly; main courses typically range from $15 to $25.

Pro Tip: Linger Eatuary has some tasty desserts, but for a memorable treat, save room for a cone from next door's unique Little Man Ice Cream shop.

THE MYSTERY OF THE DENVER MINT STICKUP

Who stole $200,000 from the Denver Mint?

The Denver Mint, said to be the most productive mint of all, has manufactured more than 300 billion coins in over a century of operation.

In 1896, Congress authorized the establishment of a full-fledged mint in Denver, buying a city block downtown for $60,000. Construction began the next year, but the mint didn't start production until 1906.

> ### THE DENVER MINT
>
> **What:** Said to be the most productive of America's four coin-manufacturing mints, the Denver Mint exhibits coins, art, and a fascinating history.
>
> **Where:** 320 W. Colfax Ave.
>
> **Cost:** Free to anyone over age 7; children under 7 not admitted
>
> **Pro Tip:** Be sure to stroll over to the back of the mint to browse its gift shop.

Among the mint's treasures is its Grand Hallway, featuring chandeliers that weigh up to 450 pounds, a terrazzo marble floor, and a magnificent white marble corridor. The hallway is capped by murals by renowned artist Vincent Aderente, representing three all-American subjects: commerce, manufacturing, and mining.

The mint's artifacts include the Millionaire Calculating Machine, a 72-pound calculator invented in 1895 and used to compute the value of gold and silver deposits; an early engraving machine; and, above the Grand Hallway, a machine gun nest built in 1934, when the mint was first used to store gold bullion.

The mint's most dramatic moment took place in 1922. At the time, the mint was used to store cash from the nearby Federal Reserve Bank. On December 18, as $200,000 was being

The Denver Mint contains many parts. The mint is a factory, manufacturing coins for the US government; a history museum that contains engaging art and artifacts; and it has been the venue for a lot of fascinating history, including a bloody bank job. Photo courtesy of Flickr, Ken Lund

transferred, a car with five masked men pulled up to the money truck. Three leaped from the car, one snatching money bags and two firing sawed-off shotguns, killing a bank guard.

Eighteen days after the daring heist, police discovered a shot-up car containing the frozen, bullet-riddled corpse of Nicholas "Chaw Jimmie" Trainor, evidently killed in the minute-long shootout.

A month later, $80,000 were recovered in Minnesota. Twelve years later, police announced they knew but would not reveal the identities of the robbers, a conspiracy of five men and two women, all of them dead or serving life imprisonment. No one was ever charged with the crime.

Among the Denver Mint's many fascinating displays is a disused machine gun nest, built 12 years too late to prevent the robbery that once riveted the city.

MOTHER CABRINI, COLORADO MIRACLE WORKER

"He who believes in Me will never thirst," Christ said. How did Mother Cabrini make that come true in Colorado?

Frances Xavier Cabrini, best known as Mother Cabrini, is the patron saint of immigrants, having been canonized by the Roman Catholic Church more than 70 years ago. In her time, she also was a worldwide evangelist and educator and a Colorado miracle worker.

Two miracles led to her beatification and canonization. Others are the subject of multiple Denver-area legends.

Mother Cabrini first came to Denver in 1902, then traveled to mines in the mountains west of the city to minister to Italian workers. Two years later, she founded the Queen of Heaven orphanage southwest of Denver.

In 1910, she launched the Queen of Heaven summer camp in the mountains about 15 miles west of downtown Denver. Three nuns managed a farm on the property consisting of a couple of barns and a springhouse, which unfortunately produced precious little water. The orphans and the

MOTHER CABRINI SHRINE

What: The Mother Cabrini Shrine, west of Denver near Golden, is a complex of statues and shrines plus the Queen of Heaven Orphanage Summer Camp; a large statue of Jesus; and a convent of the Missionary Sisters of the Sacred Heart of Jesus.

Where: 20189 Cabrini Blvd., Golden

Cost: Free

Pro Tip: Pilgrims climb the 373-step stairway that follows Mother Cabrini's original path up Mount Vernon.

In 1912, Mother Cabrini started taking her nuns for mountain picnics. A north Denver fire department captain loaned his horses for the excursions, saying, "As long as Mother Cabrini is with our fire horses, there never has been nor never will be a fire in north Denver." There never was. Photos courtesy of Wikimedia Commons

sisters were forced to carry water up a steep slope from the bottom of the canyon below.

In 1912, Mother Cabrini visited the camp to direct the construction of a stone dormitory for the orphans, and the thirsty nuns begged for help. A miracle ensued.

One account says Mother Cabrini directed the sisters to dig under a rock. There they found an underground stream. Other versions of the tale say she struck the earth with her cane and water gushed forth. Another variant says she began moving the rock herself.

Today the stream still flows; it is part of the Mother Cabrini Shrine near Golden.

The Stone House, built by hand by the nuns and orphans, is on the National Register of Historic Places.

Cabrini shrines dot the United States. Chicago's National Shrine of Saint Frances Xavier Cabrini marks the spot where she died in 1917. Her body was reinterred in another shrine in New York City.

MATTIE SILKS, HER HOUSE OF MIRRORS, AND THE NAKED DUEL

Did famed madam Mattie Silks fight a topless pistol duel?

In 1877, Denver was just 19 years old and bursting with miners and cowboys with dollars to spend.

One night that year, well-known Denver madams Kate Fulton and Mattie Silks had a little too much to drink. Insults were exchanged, a fistfight broke out, and in the ensuing brawl, somebody broke Fulton's nose. Concerned that the cops might get involved, Fulton took the next train to Kansas City.

Come morning, Silks, unafraid and undeterred, filed a complaint against Fulton with the Denver district attorney.

There rested the history of the so-called duel until a so-called journalist named Forbes Parkhill in 1950 researched the melee for a book he was writing and converted it into a gun duel between Fulton and Silks.

As time went by, the two ladies lost their shirts, and the nonexistent duel became immortalized as the Nude Duel.

Meanwhile, back in actual history, Mattie Silks resumed her status as one of the most prominent madams on the "Row," a boulevard of brothels on what is now Market Street.

The battle between Mattie Silks and Kate Fulton took place in what was then Denver Park, a wooded area adjacent to the city. Today it is popular Confluence Park.

Mattie Silks, born Martha Ready in Pennsylvania, owned a brothel in Dodge City, Kansas, before heading west to Denver to profit from the mining boom. Here she became the legendary "Queen of Denver's Red Light District." Photo courtesy of Wikimedia Commons

THE HOUSE OF MIRRORS

What: Legendary Denver madam Mattie Silks became even more of a legend when an imaginative journalist invented what became known as the Naked Duel.

Where: 1942 Market St.

Cost: Free to see; Neon Baby, which like the House of Mirrors has a mirrored ceiling, is "moderately priced."

Pro Tip: A tour of Market Street yields great historical riches, all part of Denver's Lower Downtown Historic District. See the blocks just north of the former House of Mirrors for numerous 19th-century buildings.

In 1889, a madam named Jennie Rogers bought a house from Silks and made it perhaps the most popular house of ill repute on the Row.

Rogers's house boasted mirrored ceilings and mirrors hung floor to ceiling, decorated with carvings of nudes. The House of Mirrors rose to rival even the chain of houses owned by Silks.

By 1911, Rogers's fortunes had fallen, and Silks was able to buy the House of Mirrors. She operated it for only four years before the law shut it down.

Today the House of Mirrors is marked by a memorial plaque, the grand façade Jennie built, and a nightclub called Neon Baby.

DENVER PLAYERS/ DENVER SUGAR'S SEEDY SAGA

Was Denver's mayor a patron of the city's most notorious brothel?

Denver Players/Denver Sugar wrote its own chapter in the colorful history of the city's seedy side.

Denver Players started as a high-rent "escort service." It ended after it took down a US District Court judge and, nearly, the city's mayor.

Founder Scottie Ewing certainly fits the definition of "colorful character."

A retired professional skier, in the early 2000s, Ewing launched Denver Players, which was said to have enjoyed the patronage of professional athletes, prominent businessmen, doctors, lawyers, and politicians.

In 2005, Ewing sold Denver Players to ex-employee Brenda Stewart and opened a similar house in another part of Denver.

CITY PARK'S FERRIL LAKE

What: An escort service turned brothel that embroiled a mayor in its controversies

Where: Denver Players at one point was surveilled by police near 17th Street and City Park's Ferril Lake.

Cost: Free

Pro Tip: Denver Players was located near the Denver Museum of Nature & Science, but we don't think that was the attraction.

Denver cathouse Denver Players was a poorly kept secret until an IRS raid made it a very public controversy that ensnared a prominent judge and, nearly, Denver's mayor.

Three-term Denver Mayor Michael Hancock was caught up in controversy over a local escort service turned house of ill repute. However, Hancock handily escaped any consequences of the Denver Players/Denver Sugar scandal. Photo courtesy of Wikipedia, Michael Johnston

Then the roof fell in. In 2008, the IRS and Denver police raided Denver Players, seizing financial, client, and appointment books.

Later, the Denver Police Department released redacted records from the raid, including about 1,300 partially obscured names and phone numbers. The ensuing scandal hit four people.

Ewing ended up serving six months of home arrest for tax evasion and paying $77,000 in back taxes. Stewart was sentenced to a year of home detention and payment of $45,000 in back taxes. Two public officials suffered pushback: Chief US District Judge Edward Nottingham resigned in 2008 following claims he had spent big money on a regular basis at Denver strip clubs and Denver Players.

Denver Mayor Michael Hancock's cell phone number in 2011 allegedly turned up in Denver Players records with his name listed as "Michael Hancook." Charges that he was a Denver Players patron faded, but were revived in 2018 when sexual harassment charges against him emerged.

In the end, neither of these charges seemed to matter much to Hancock or Denver voters, who in 2019 returned him to office for a third term with 56 percent of the vote. Hancock's secret, if he has one, seems safe.

HOW A "MIRACULOUS" DEAL SAVED A HALF-HIDDEN GEM

How did Holy Ghost Church end up in the shadow of a downtown skyscraper?

Denver's most beautiful church interior is hiding in plain sight.

Holy Ghost Church, downtown at 1900 California Street, sits in the shadow of the 43-story 1999 Broadway office tower.

In the early 1980s, the church sold its air rights. The result combined the church's preservation with a deal its monsignor called "miraculous," in effect selling the rectory and garage for $8.5 million.

Famed Denver-based Fentress Architects sought to maximize the church's triangular-shaped block by designing a wraparound glass skyscraper, completed in 1985.

Monsignor Charles B. Woodrich, better known as Father Woody, negotiated this miraculous deal while innovating a new era in care for the poor.

Father Woody opened the church to the homeless in 1982, during an epochal Denver snowstorm. He also instituted an annual Christmas party where he fed more than 3,000 while giving away $10 bills, and later $20 bills.

Father Woody died in November 1991. The $1.5 million Father Woody's Haven of Hope homeless services center,

---

Downtown's Holy Ghost Church was designed by distinguished Denver architect Jules Benedict, who designed more than two dozen Colorado structures now on the National Register of Historic Places.

The strange conjunction of Holy Ghost Church, a Renaissance-style construction, and the 43-story 1999 Broadway office tower, happened for a variety of reasons. One was the odd fact that downtown Denver is platted at a right angle to the rest of the city, making the church's block triangular. Photo courtesy of Wikipedia, Xnatedawgx

HOLY GHOST CHURCH

What: A modern Renaissance-style masterpiece, today is accompanied by the looming, 43-story 1999 Broadway office building.

Where: 1900 California St.

Cost: Free

Pro Tip: Holy Ghost Church is a short walk to numerous Denver landmarks, such as Sakura Square (the center of Colorado's Japanese community), and the popular 16th Street Mall.

located about two miles from Holy Ghost Church, opened in 2007.

Holy Ghost Church was designed by renowned Denver architect Jules Jacques Benois Benedict in 1923.

The church remained unfinished until 1943, when contributions by heiress Helen Bonfils enabled its completion.

Benedict designed a blend of Spanish and Italian Renaissance architecture. The exterior features a 110-foot tower with a six-foot bronze cross, blond bricks, cream-colored trim, and a green tile roof reflected in the finish of the skyscraper next door.

The interior walls and columns are made of about 300 tons of Colorado travertine marble. The nave features ruby, cream, and dark pink marble with floors of inlaid brass, beige Botticino marble, and pink travertine.

But don't be misled by all that brass and stone: the church has a spacious feel, as befits an architectural gem half-hidden in the heart of Denver.

GHOSTLY GUESTS AT THE LAVISH BROWN PALACE HOTEL

How does the Brown Palace exemplify Denver history and luxury . . . and spooks?

The Brown Palace Hotel and Spa is the crown jewel of downtown Denver, conjoining the city's history, mystery, and luxury.

The Brown Palace Hotel is a gem of architecture and interior decor. It also is famous for ghosts, spooky phone calls from empty rooms, and a legendary tunnel.

The Brown Palace was built between 1888 and 1892 by Henry Cordes Brown. Brown had brought his family to Colorado in 1859 via ox team. (Brown is not to be confused with Denver's then-power couple, J. J. Brown and "Unsinkable" Molly Brown.)

The Brown Palace rapidly earned fame as one of the world's exclusive hostelries. Its guest list has included five US presidents from Theodore Roosevelt to Ronald Reagan, Queen Marie of Romania, and Denver's most notorious conman, "Soapy" Smith (see p. 140).

In a hipper vein, the Brown hosted the Beatles in 1964. Other musicians followed: the Rolling Stones, Bruce Springsteen, Cindy Lauper, Jon Bon Jovi, Metallica, Pearl Jam, and Taylor Swift all have stayed there.

Years ago, the Brown offered the sale of rail tickets in its lobby. Today, guests say they still see spectral ticket agents and travelers.

Like a number of buildings on the periphery of downtown Denver, the triangular Brown Palace Hotel sits on a triangle-shaped lot. This is due to the odd fact that downtown Denver is set at a right angle to the rest of the city. Photo courtesy of Wikimedia Commons

THE BROWN PALACE HOTEL AND SPA

What: Downtown Denver's ritziest—and second-oldest—hotel

Where: 321 17th St.

Cost: Prices vary, starting at about $140 for a single room for two adults and going up to about $240 for a suite.

Pro Tip: The Brown features history tours, free for guests and $20 for the general public.

The hotel's traditions include a daily formal tea, punctuated annually by tea with the National Western Stock Show Grand Champion Steer.

The hotel has a tunnel to an annex across the street. It is also rumored to have had a tunnel linking it to a brothel across the street in the Navarre Building, now home to the American Museum of Western Art. That tunnel might have been filled in, or it might never have existed.

The Brown long has been haunted—by a spectral orchestra, mysterious travelers, and a longtime resident named Louise Crawford Hill. Hill lived in the hotel for 15 years until her death in 1955. It is said that she continues to make telephone calls to the Brown's switchboard.

AN ARCHITECTURAL AND ASTRONOMICAL MARVEL

How did a marvel of 19th-century astronomy wind up 20 minutes by car from downtown Denver?

The University of Denver's Chamberlin Observatory is a showpiece of urban architecture and astronomy, scientific antiquity, and contemporary utility.

In other words, with 95 percent of its original parts intact, the observatory's 1894 refractor telescope still works.

Chamberlin Observatory is the centerpiece of Denver's Observatory Park, located a couple of blocks from the University of Denver. (The observatory belongs to the university, which in 1950 donated the two-block park to Denver.)

The park itself is a gem in the middle of the city. The observatory building is a beautiful Richardsonian Romanesque domed structure of red sandstone block and rounded arches constructed in 1888. It was a gift to the university by Humphrey Barker Chamberlin, a real estate millionaire who lost his fortune, his health, and his life after the Silver Panic of 1893. Chamberlin donated $56,000, a sum worth about $1.5 million today.

It's paired with a nearby Student Observatory building, which was built at the same time as the main building and is still used for student projects.

But the centerpiece of the park is Chamberlin Observatory and its magnificent Clark-Saegmuller refractor telescope.

Chamberlin Observatory's creation is credited to its benefactor, H. B. Chamberlin, and the University of Denver's first professor of astronomy, Dr. Herbert Howe.

Denver's Robert Roeschlaub, one of Colorado's first licensed architects, designed the Chamberlin Observatory building after the larger Goodsell Observatory in Northfield, Minnesota. Its Romanesque-style architecture, with sturdy weight-bearing walls, was especially apropos for an observatory, which needs to hold a telescope absolutely steady. Photo courtesy of Wikimedia Commons

CHAMBERLIN OBSERVATORY AND OBSERVATORY PARK

What: A beautiful example of late 19th-century architecture and astronomy

Where: 2930 East Warren Ave.

Cost: Adults, $4; children, $3

Pro Tip: For an online preview, see www.youtube.com/watch?v=P85JwkETecA.

More than 26 feet long, with a 20-inch aperture, the telescope was constructed at the height of a trend toward refraction telescopes, shortly before the reflection kind took over, and before electricity reached Denver. When it was installed in 1894, its telescope was the fifth largest in the United States.

Today, its observational powers are enhanced by its mile-high altitude, just as they were when it was opened, while struggling with modern urban light pollution.

Public tours of the telescope also began in 1894. They continue today, for just $3 for children and $4 for adults.

DENVER'S ALL-TIME CON KING

How did Jefferson "Soapy" Smith earn his nickname?

Jefferson Randolph "Soapy" Smith—amid a crowded field of worthy competitors—stands out as Denver history's unrivaled conman.

When it comes to swindling on a vast scale, Soapy Smith reigned supreme as the "king of the frontier confidence men."

Smith spent the best years of his career during Denver's frontier days, when the young city was a roiling mess of con games, hookers, piggish politicians, and shady businessmen.

Smith was far from a lone trickster. He was a crime overlord in Denver, then Creede (about 250 miles southwest of Denver), and then Denver again, from 1884 to 1895. When the law and other misfortunes caught up with him in Colorado, he flimflammed in Skagway, Alaska, from 1896 to 1898.

Soapy Smith earned his nickname through a con that became a steady earner for him and his gang.

After making a handsome living cheating at cards and excelling at the shell game, Soapy hit pay dirt after developing what the Denver newspapers called "the prize soap racket."

Soapy would set up a table with a pile of bars of soap wrapped in paper, announcing that one in ten $5 bars was wrapped in $20 or $50. After palming the bills, a shill in the crowd would exclaim that he had bought a bar wrapped in money. Then Soapy would announce that one remaining bar

---

Soapy Smith ably summed up his life in a sort of epitaph: "Upon the world he made his mark, and from him we learn how not to be one."

In 1894, Colorado's new governor fired three corrupt Denver officials. They barricaded themselves in city hall with other officials, and Soapy. The governor wheeled up a cannon and Gatling guns; Soapy and gang grabbed rifles and dynamite bombs and headed for the roof. The City Hall War ended peacefully, however. Photo courtesy of Wikimedia Commons

EUCLID HALL BAR & KITCHEN

What: The brief life and violent death of Denver's con king

Where: The Euclid Hall Bar & Kitchen, formerly Soapy Smith's Eagle Bar, located in one of Soapy's former gambling halls, 1317 14th St.

Cost: Menu items range from grits with white miso and scallions for $4 to ham-brined pork chop, $25.

Pro Tip: For a taste of Soapy's old stomping grounds, talk a stroll through Larimer Square, the 1400 block of Larimer Street.

was wrapped in a $100 bill, sell out the remaining soap bars, and vanish.

His soapy empire prospered. For a time, Soapy controlled almost all the gambling in Denver. Later, he controlled all the gambling in Creede.

Smith met his death at age 37 in a shootout in Skagway in 1898. His last words were, "My God, don't shoot!"

For once, he failed to fool anyone.

HIDDEN BEAUTIES

Did you know many of Denver's most beautiful parks are outside the city limits?

Denver's regal parks system can be divided in two parts because many of its most magnificent parks are not to be found in the City and County of Denver.

We mean the Denver Mountain Parks, more than 4,000 acres of parkland outside the city limits comprising 22 developed parks, plus open space.

For instance, beautiful 2,413-acre Genesee Park—complete with buffalo herd and the magnificent Chief Hosa Lodge, built in 1918—actually is located in Jefferson County.

Then there's Echo Lake Park in Clear Creek County, 33 miles west and more than 5,000 feet up from Denver. The park, at the foot of 14,271-foot Mount Evans, features the Echo Lake Lodge restaurant and gift shop, built in 1926. Of course it also contains Echo Lake, a glacial lake at an altitude of 10,600 feet.

From the sublime to the truly tiny is the smallest park in the mountain parks system, Colorow Point Park on Lookout Mountain in Golden.

Colorow Point Park, named for famed Ute Mountain tribe chief Colorow, occupies just a bit more than one-third of an acre. But at an elevation of about 7,500 feet, its views are stunning, spanning from Rocky Mountain National Park to Clear Creek and the Continental Divide.

The mountain parks system contains many more unique gems. Summit Lake Park, 160 acres at 12,840 feet on the way

---

Denver launched its mountain parks system in 1912. Today the system encompasses 46 properties (some closed to the public) from rolling prairie to alpine tundra.

Echo Lake Park lies by the Mount Evans Scenic Byway, the same road that leads to Summit Lake Park, a fellow Denver mountain park, and the summit of Mount Evans, Colorado's 12th highest peak. The byway is the highest paved road in North America. Photo courtesy of Wikimedia Commons, Matt Wright

MOUNTAIN PARKS

What: Denver Mountain Parks have something for every outdoors lover.

Where: In and around Denver

Cost: Most mountain parks are free.

Pro Tip: Denver's famous buffalo herd often can be seen from one of the area's busiest highways, Interstate 70, but it's best to stop off and visit their home, the Buffalo Herd Nature Preserve.

to the top of Mount Evans, contains untouched tundra and wildflowers found nowhere else outside the Arctic Circle.

Red Rocks Park and its spectacular rock formations include America's No. 1 outdoor amphitheater (see p. 74).

Finally, there's the exception that proves the rule: Winter Park Resort, Colorado's first ski major area. It is not part of the mountain parks system, but it is owned by Denver and operated by Denver-based Alterra Mountain Company.

200 MILES OF SWEEPING VIEWS

Where do you go to find Denver's finest view of the Rockies?

Denver is justly proud of its vast and seemingly omnipresent city parks system. Mestizo-Curtis Park, built in 1868, is the oldest. City Park, modeled after New York City's Central Park, is the largest.

And Inspiration Point Park in northwest Denver is the breathtaking-est.

Visitors pretty much have to go out of their way to avoid remarkable views of downtown Denver and/or the sweep of the Front Range of the Rocky Mountains. (The best place to go to ignore both views, paradoxically, is downtown Denver, where skyscrapers obliterate the view of each other as well as the mountain landscape.)

Among this abundance of awe-inspiring views, Inspiration Point Park stands out. At 25.5 acres, Inspiration Point is a smallish park on a bluff in northwest Denver about 11 miles from the Rockies. Simply put, it is not too close and not too far from the sweep of the Front Range, and no building or other object blocks its view.

That's how the view extends nearly 200 miles from north to south, taking in numerous massive mountains of 14,000 feet-plus (called "14ers" by Coloradans).

From south to north the most prominent of these are the most famous, 14,115-foot Pikes Peak; the most accessible,

Eleven miles from the mountains and seven miles from the Colorado State Capitol, Inspiration Point Park displays the vast Rocky Mountains better than any other city park.

Inspiration Point Park features panoramic views of 200 miles of the Rocky Mountains, plus pleasant walking and hiking trails, ancient evergreens, friendly picnic grounds, and plenty of walls and benches for climbing and sitting. Photo courtesy of Wikimedia Commons, Jeffrey Beall

Mount Evans, whose 14,271-foot summit can be climbed by car in warm weather; and the most dramatic, Longs Peak, 14,259 feet.

Inspiration Point Park was inspired by the 1906 plan for the beautification of Denver by Charles Mulford Robinson, a pioneering urban planner and proponent of the City Beautiful movement. The park was designed in 1910 and opened three years later. It offers easy walking and running trails, ample picnic grounds, and that fabulous view.

INSPIRATION POINT PARK

What: Unrivaled views of the Front Range of the Rockies

Where: 4901 Sheridan Blvd.

Cost: Free

Pro Tip: Inspiration Point Park has a reputation as a lover's lane, so consider yourself warned.

THE GRUESOME TALE OF THREE PROMINENT DENVER PARKS

Are three of Denver's most popular parks really built on a boneyard?

Denver's Cheesman Park and Congress Park, as well as the Denver Botanic Gardens, are central to the city's history and culture and well worth a visit. They offer timeless architecture, flowing lawns and towering shade trees, thrilling concerts, and important botanical research.

And all three are built on a graveyard.

In 1858, Denver's first cemetery opened. Congress converted its 160 acres into federal land in 1872, by which time it was called Denver City Cemetery.

Then, Denver's population exploded to 106,713 people in 1890 from 35,629 in 1880.

The city persuaded Congress to let it convert the cemetery to parkland. Denver named the place Congress Park in gratitude.

Denver developed a plan to move the roughly 5,000 graves elsewhere. Work on the grisly project began in 1893. It was a revolting failure. The city fired the project's manager before the corpses could be shifted. Some never were.

Time passed, and the cemetery's territory was divided into three.

Denver's old Mount Prospect Cemetery (also known by various other names) was built on ground said originally to have been a burial site for the Arapaho Indians and, later, pioneer families.

Denver's Cheesman Park's renowned Cheesman Memorial Pavilion, once affectionately known as the "Temple in the Sun," was built in 1910 from Colorado Yule marble. Much of its original design was lost in a 1970s reconstruction, but it remains impressive. Photo courtesy of Pixaby

DENVER'S HAUNTED PARKS AND GARDENS

What: Three parks built atop Denver's first cemetery—and numerous corpses

Where: Denver Botanic Gardens: 1007 York St.; Cheesman Park, 1599 E. 8th Ave.; Congress Park, 914 S. Columbine St.

Cost: The parks are free. Denver Botanic Gardens: adults, $15; seniors, military, and veterans, $11.50; children and students, $11; children two and under, free.

Pro Tip: Denver Botanic Gardens actually comprises three separate parks: one in central Denver's Cheesman Park neighborhood; another, the Denver Botanic Gardens at Chatfield, near Chatfield State Park; and the third, Mount Goliath, a high-altitude wildflower garden. Each is different. All are beautiful.

Today, 80-acre Cheesman Park is the crown jewel of Denver's Capitol Hill neighborhood, the city's central residential district. Its landscaping and columned pavilion are world renowned.

The Denver Botanic Gardens next door comprises a world-class collection of cold-climate plants, a concert amphitheater, and the first-ever Xeriscape Demonstration Garden.

Across the street lies Congress Park, the name of a neighborhood and also a city park that contains a playground, picnic grounds, and the city's communications center.

Of course, these three venues are said to be haunted. Scans with ground-penetrating radar have shown numerous graves extant. In 2008, work on a new parking garage for the botanic gardens revealed an old grave. In 2010, repairs of Cheesman Park's irrigation system uncovered four well-preserved skeletons.

Underfoot, uncounted bodies are trod on daily. No one minds. Come visit. You won't mind either.

DENVER, THE MILE HIGH CITY, MEASURES UP

How did the Colorado State Capitol get three mile-high markers?

Scads of Denver place-names contain "Mile High" or a variant, probably the most famous being the old Mile High Stadium, nowadays called Empower Field at Mile High.

The condensed version is "5,280," the number of feet in a mile and Denver's altitude above sea level. (There are 1,609 meters in a mile.)

Denver hosts many notable places where 5,280 feet have been precisely measured or publicly commemorated.

Some of these come and go. The Denver Nuggets basketball team, for instance, has painted "5280" on its basketball court at the Pepsi Center.

Some are not precisely measured. For the sake of discomfiting rivals, the Denver Broncos football team affixed a sign above the visitors' locker room doors at Empower Field warning: "Elevation 5,280 Feet Above Sea Level."

A couple of more permanent, more scientifically measured shrines to Denver's altitude are worth a mention.

Coors Field, the home ballpark of the Colorado Rockies baseball club, has a seating capacity of 46,897. All the seats are

COLORADO STATE CAPITOL

What: Lots of places and things are named after Denver's dizzying distance above sea level.

Where: The Colorado State Capitol: 200 East Colfax Ave.

Cost: Free

Pro Tip: The capitol's stairs are the steps that launched a thousand selfies.

Dozens of Denver businesses and other institutions are named either "Mile High" or a derivative, "5280." If you can stand the effects of high altitude, a good one to visit is the City Park Mile High Loop, a three-mile run at 5,280 feet. Photo courtesy of Wikimedia Commons, J. Miers

dark green except the 5,280-foot, 865-seat purple 20th row of the upper deck.

The Colorado State Capitol sits on a hill providing a panoramic view of the mountains, downtown Denver, and the Denver Civic Center. A steep flight of steps leads to the capitol entrance.

The fifteenth step is carved with the notation "One Mile Above Sea Level." This is the step that purported to show a mile of altitude from 1909 to 1969. That year, students from Colorado State University re-measured the steps, moving the spot up three steps. Finally, in 2003 another measurement was taken using more modern standards. A brass medallion was installed on the 13th step to mark the place. The difference between the low step and the high step is about five feet, or about 1.5 meters.

Denver has numerous nicknames—Queen City of the Plains; Queen City of the West; Wall Street of the West—but the Mile High City is by far the most popular.

WHERE TO FIND THE WORLD'S BEST CLOCK

What clock loses one-tenth of a nanosecond per day?

Your wristwatch won't tell you the exact time. Your computer won't, nor will your cell phone.

If you want to know the exact time—the really, really exact time—go to Boulder. There, 27 miles from the Colorado State Capitol, is the National Institute of Standards and Technology's Time and Frequency Division.

This is the place where they build the most accurate clocks on Earth.

Take the case of the atomic clock they call NIST-F1. In the year 2000, its uncertainty was about 1 × 10–15, meaning that it would lose about 0.1 nanosecond per day. (A nanosecond equals one-billionth of a second.)

But this wasn't good enough for the physicists at the Time and Frequency Division, so they kept (to use the scientific term) messing with the clock. By January 2013, its "uncertainty" reached about 3 × 10–16. This means 100 million years would go by before it would gain or lose a second.

Then, in 2014, they developed NIST-F2. NIST-F1 remains the nation's main timekeeper.

Actually, you don't need to go to Boulder to enjoy the world's most accurate timepiece. You have handy alternatives.

One is to be found online: the website called time.gov, a venture of the National Institute of Standards and Technology

---

Female scientists have played a central role at NIST. Katharine Blodgett Gebbie worked there until her 2016 death, overseeing the work of four Nobel Prize winners.

The NIST atomic clocks use lasers to send cesium atoms through a microwave chamber. The microwaves cause the atoms to emit photons. The microwave frequency that maximizes the emission of photons is used to define the second. Photo courtesy of NIST

and the US Naval Observatory. (Click on "About This Site" for all kinds of interesting information, including links to downloadable software that allows you to set your computer to official NIST-F1 time.)

We should note that NIST Time and Frequency Division scientist Dave Wineland shared the 2012 Nobel Prize in Physics for quantum systems research that has direct bearing on developing better atomic clocks.

NATIONAL INSTITUTE OF STANDARDS AND TECHNOLOGY

What: Boulder's National Institute of Standards and Technology hosts the world's most accurate clocks.

Where: 325 Broadway, Boulder

Cost: Alas, the National Institute of Standards and Technology in Boulder stopped offering public tours, citing "staffing and security requirements."

Pro Tip: In addition to time.gov, you can access atomic clock time by calling (303) 499-7111 or (808) 335-4363. Calls from landlines suffer from delays of less than 30 milliseconds.

SHHH . . . HERE'S A GUIDE TO DENVER'S SECRET BARS

How can you find Denver's hidden bars?

The Mile High City has at least a half-dozen hidden bars but, really, who knows?

These saloons can be pretty hard to find. They tend not to advertise their whereabouts, sometimes not even on the Internet.

Millers & Rossi (M&R) is an art gallery at 3542 Walnut St. in the terribly hip RiNo Arts District. M&R features paintings, sculptures, photography, and mixed media. Pass through what it calls a "hidden picture frame-esque door," and you enter a darkly lit, fully appointed, richly atmospheric bar.

Patrons enter Williams & Graham, 3160 Tejon St., through a bookstore and bookcase. Once inside, they find themselves in an intimate, 60-seat bar and restaurant.

Green Russell, situated in famed Larimer Square, is easy to find once you locate the sign for the Wednesday's Pie shop. Ask at the shop for directions if need be. If not, descend a flight of stairs to Green Russell, a "speakeasy" styled after actual speakeasies. One brilliant stroke: You must use a phone booth to make cell phone calls. Find it if you can at 1422 Larimer St.

DENVER'S SECRET SALOONS

What: Like an online adventure game, bars that make themselves scarce can be fun.

Where: Various locations around Denver

Cost: Entrance is invariably free, if sometimes difficult. After that, it's up to you.

Pro Tip: Get reservations if you can. It can be tough to get into these bars.

The Cooper Lounge puts patrons above, but not in, bustling Union Station, overlooking the historic train station's Great Hall. It's connected to the station on one end and the Crawford Hotel on the other. Photo courtesy of Cooper Lounge

A few more hidden bars:

Retrograde is hidden inside an ice cream shop, Frozen Matter. Enter through a freezer door at 530 E. 19th Ave.

You'll find the B&GC (said to stand for "Boys and Girls Club") in the basement of the Halcyon Hotel, 245 Columbine St., down a flight of stairs behind a door marked "Stair 3." Text for reservations: (720) 925-8598. Good luck.

The Cooper Lounge hides in plain sight on the mezzanine of Denver's Union Station, at 1701 Wynkoop St. To get there, look for a desk next to a velvet rope on the south side of the station. Ask for admittance. Once you get there, enjoy the giant 28-feet-high windows, soaring views, and retro decor.

Hidden bars sometimes are called speakeasies, but a speakeasy by definition is a bar that serves illegal beverages. That you will not find.

DENVER'S OLDEST HOTEL . . . AND ITS ART DECO BAR

Who did you say used to lift a toast in the Cruise Room?

The Oxford Hotel, Denver's oldest hotel, was founded in 1891. It contains the Cruise Room, the city's oldest lounge, opened in 1933. But both are so much more than merely old, and both are flush with ghosts . . . and other secrets.

The Cruise Room is what every other Denver bar wishes it was. It opened the day after Prohibition ended. It was designed in 1933 by architect Gilbert Charles Jaka to emulate what today is known as the Queen Mary Observation Bar & Art Deco Lounge (still serving on the famous ship in Long Beach, California). Its marble floors, original chrome, art deco murals, and neon lighting propel patrons back in time.

The Cruise Room was remodeled in 2012 by developer Dana Crawford, the force behind Denver's Larimer Square, Union Station, and so much else in the city that is good and true.

Crawford restored the bar's magical reddish lighting, its orange walls with their Art Deco murals, and much else, but there was one restoration no one will undertake, ever.

Secrets? The Cruise Room has secret tunnels and panes from the Prohibition days, some say. That might or might not be.

In 2016, the Oxford celebrated its 125th anniversary by offering the Oxford Laws Million Dollar VIP Package, featuring Denver-based Laws Whiskey House's Oxford 1891 Batch #2 Four Grain Straight Bourbon.

The Cruise Room is a long, narrow space filled with atmosphere and history. Perhaps due to its scarlet lighting and orange walls, Art Deco murals and retro uniforms, it has a time-capsule feel. Photo courtesy of Flickr, Chris Bartle

OXFORD HOTEL AND CRUISE ROOM

What: Denver's oldest hotel and oldest lounge make an unbeatable combination.

Where: 1600 17th St.

Cost: Rooms range upward from the $160s per night; suites are similar, with a higher ceiling. Prices are extremely variable.

Pro Tip: The Oxford Hotel is in Denver's LoDo district (short for "lower downtown"). Union Station is a short walk.

What is not disputed is that the room's murals of toasts around the world once included Adolph Hitler and Benito Mussolini. Whoops. These were painted over sometime in the 1940s.

Crawford renovated—rescued might be a better word—the Oxford Hotel starting in 1980. Yet she failed to eradicate its restless spirits. The Oxford features a murderous woman named Florence Montague who continues to appear in a third-floor room. Also, watch for a deceased postal worker who persists in delivering mail to the Cruise Room.

So enjoy the Oxford Hotel and its Cruise Room. And beware.

A SELF-SECRET WAY TO SEE DENVER'S UNION STATION

What remains of the old Union Station?

Union Station, hub of Denver's "multimodal" transportation system, was built in 1881, rebuilt in 1894, and reconstructed and reopened in 2014.

The interior of the old Union Station was impressive, 65 feet high and lit by chandeliers eight feet across. But by the time the 21st century dawned, it had become pretty badly beaten up. The chandeliers had been replaced by tacky fluorescent lights, and almost all its 10-foot-long heated benches, filled with asbestos, had to go.

Then Denver redevelopment doyenne Dana Crawford took a hand. In 2008, she and an investment group bid on the rebirth of the station. They won their bid in 2011, transforming the dilapidated dump into a bustling hub bristling with bars, shops, and restaurants. The station's hotel was named the Crawford Hotel in honor of the woman who almost single-handedly transformed Lower Downtown Denver.

The 21st-century renovators invested $54 million in the station while more than $1 billion has been sunk into the surrounding neighborhood.

UNION STATION

What: The restoration of Union Station combines the best of the old rail terminus with modern design.

Where: 1700 Wynkoop St., Denver

Cost: Free

Pro Tip: Need something to read on the train or bus? See the Union Station branch of the Tattered Cover, Denver's premier bookstore.

Union Station has been rebuilt many times in the past 140 or so years. Architectural drawings of the 1914 interior renovation are on display between the third and fourth floors. Photo courtesy of Wikimedia Commons, Darkshark0159

Union Station's interior today doesn't look much like the prior version—but if you know where to look, there is still a lot of the old station to see.

Those 10-foot benches? Two remain along the north side of the Great Hall.

Those giant chandeliers? They're long gone, but the new chandeliers were modeled on the originals. They are said to be even larger than the old ones.

The station's ticket window is original. The old one was found under a layer of drywall and refurbished.

Some original interior decor remains, such as ornaments along the walls in the shape of Colorado's state flower, the Rocky Mountain Columbine.

So enjoy Denver's Union Station, one of America's resplendent rail terminals—especially if you know where to look.

For a self-guided tour of the glory days of Union Station, see the displays of old tickets, coins, and other souvenirs on the second floor.

THE MONEY MUSEUM AND ITS FREE BAGS OF BILLS

Have you ever wanted to see $30 million in cash?

The Federal Reserve Bank of Kansas City Denver Branch. Could anything sound duller?

How about a parking lot tour? A visit to Idaho's biggest potato field?

The Denver bank is the second-largest branch of the Federal Reserve Bank of Kansas City. But the Federal Reserve Bank of Kansas City only has three branches, so big deal, right?

To add insult, the bank is located in an off-putting 1968 building, which replaced the classical federal architecture of its 1925 headquarters.

Yet the Federal Reserve Bank in Denver is actually pretty cool and well worth a quick visit, especially if you have children in tow. It's more fun when combined with a tour of the Denver Mint, a 15-minute walk away. That's due to this often-overlooked institution's 7,000-square-foot Money Museum.

In 2010, the bank decided to do something about an underused 10,000-square-foot space. Down came boring dark wood panels; up went attractive backlighting and 15-foot-high ceilings. The room overlooks Denver's bustling 16th Street Mall. In addition to the Money Museum, the renovation added a theater and a kitchen.

The Federal Reserve's Denver branch opened in 1918. It moved in 1925 and again in 1968, when an urban renewal project obliterated the old bank.

The Denver branch opened in 1918 in a building that was too cold and so small that it forced the bank to store currency at the Denver Mint, paving the way for the mint robbery of 1922 (see p. 126). Photo courtesy of Wikimedia Commons, Xnatedawgx

DENVER MONEY MUSEUM

What: This museum will show you more cash than you have ever seen.

Where: 1020 16th St.

Cost: Free

Pro Tip: No reservations are needed to visit the museum, but be sure to bring identification—a driver's license or passport. A passport is essential if you have a foreign driver's license.

The Money Museum's highlights are a real $100,000 dollar bill and an exhibit of $30 million – surely the most cash most of us will ever see. Other displays include an informative section on counterfeiting and historic currency.

The museum shows children the meaning of money and of savings and interest. Adults will enjoy the museum most if they have a particular interest in money or banking. Departing visitors are given a bag of shredded cash, fun if not enriching.

IN WITH THE OLD, IN WITH THE NEW

What hotel lobby is the "most beautiful room in Denver"?

The Renaissance Denver Downtown City Center Hotel could be called a bank disguised as a hotel. In 2014, it rose from the ashes of the old Colorado National Bank, whose storied downtown Denver branch had been constructed in 1915 and abandoned in 1998.

The old bank was a spectacular building. Both inside and out, it used white Yule Marble quarried in Colorado, the source of the marble used for the Tomb of the Unknown Soldier and the Lincoln Memorial. The neoclassical building was designed by renowned Denver architects Fisher & Fisher and dubbed "the bank that looks like a bank."

Its lobby, a three-story atrium, is dominated by 16 murals collectively called "Indian Memories," including the colossal "Happy Hunting Ground" capping its main entrance.

The murals were painted by Colorado native Allen Tupper True, whose art also adorns the Brown Palace Hotel.

The hotel's renovation and refurbishment burnished the lobby into what *The Denver Post* called possibly "the most beautiful room in Denver," rivaled only by the Brown Palace and the Cathedral Basilica of the Immaculate Conception near the State Capitol.

The Renaissance Denver hotel has three layers. The bottom structure is the original 1915 bank, and above it is a 1925 edition. The hotel added a third floor in 2014.

Pictured here is the entrance to one of three giant bank vaults ingeniously converted into spacious meeting rooms by the Renaissance Denver Downtown City Center Hotel's Denver-based developer Stonebridge Cos. Photo courtesy of Flickr, Davis Staedtler

THE RENAISSANCE DENVER DOWNTOWN CITY CENTER HOTEL

What: The Renaissance Denver Downtown City Center Hotel rescued an architectural wonder that was on its way to ruin.

Where: 918 17th St.

Cost: Free to visit.

Pro Tip: The hotel boasts Colorado's only illy Caffè, serving its famous espresso and other coffees as well as breakfast, lunch, and desserts.

Today the 230-room hotel capitalizes on some of the old bank lobby's most spectacular features, notably three giant old bank vaults.

The vaults help explain why it took so long for the building to be converted from its former derelict state: They were too enormous to be removed without destroying the lobby around them. The hotel simply converted them to meeting rooms. Now it has 6,000 square feet of meeting room space in the middle of the Denver financial district.

The hotel also has a "history wall" and a lobby bar that provides an enviable vantage point from which to admire the city's most beautiful room.

THE BOULDER DUSHANBE TEAHOUSE'S LONG, STRANGE, MAGNIFICENT TRIP

How did an authentic Tajik tea house wind up in Boulder?

If you've ever wanted to take a brief vacation in old Tajikistan without the inconvenience of actually traveling there, check out the Boulder Dushanbe Teahouse.

The what?

As if you didn't know, Dushanbe is the capital of the Republic of Tajikistan, a landlocked nation of 9.2 million and a former republic of the Soviet Union in Central Asia.

Boulder hosts its Tajik tea house, authentic in every detail, just a few blocks south of the popular Boulder Mall.

How the city ended up with a Tajik tea house is a long, strange story.

The tale began because Boulder and Dushanbe are sister cities.

In 1987, the mayor of Dushanbe visited Boulder and proclaimed that his city would celebrate the relationship through the gift of a tea house.

Boulder reciprocated through various exchanges and the development of a cyber cafe in Dushanbe, which opened in 2009.

In addition to all its other virtues, the Boulder Dushanbe Teahouse is in a wonderful location, a few minutes from the busy Boulder Mall and other attractions.

A look at Tajikistan's history reveals just how generous its gift really was. In 1987, when Mayor Maksud Ikramov offered Boulder the tea house, his nation was four years away from independence from the USSR and just five years from the start of a devastating civil war. Photo courtesy of Flickr

Meantime, 40 Tajik artisans and craftspeople took two years to fashion the tea house (without power tools), dismantle it, and fit it into crates. In 1990, they shipped it to Boulder.

There the tea house remained for eight years, in its crates, while Boulder argued over funding, zoning, insuring, and other thorny American-style issues.

Finally, it opened on Boulder's 13th Street, next to the Boulder Museum of Contemporary Art, across the street from the Central Park band shell, and right by rippling Boulder Creek.

The tea house is exotic and magnificent. Its exterior features eight ceramic "Tree of Life" panels and a rose garden. Its interior centers on a fountain celebrating a 12th-century poem, "The Seven Beauties," and eight carved white panels. Its carved ceiling and 12 cedar columns are intricate and enchanting. The restaurant also serves 100 kinds of tea.

BOULDER DUSHANBE TEAHOUSE

What: The Boulder Dushanbe Teahouse took about four years to build and almost nine years to install.

Where: 1770 13th St., Boulder

Cost: Free to enter. Tea and meals are extra.

Pro Tip: Call 24 hours in advance, (303) 442-4993, to make reservations for afternoon tea featuring premium tea and special pastries. Served from 3:00 pm to 5:00 pm; $24 per person, or $15 per child under age 9.

REACH-OUT-AND-TOUCH-IT VIEW

Where, 30 miles from the State Capitol, is the best view of the Continental Divide?

It's hard to avoid magnificent mountain views from Denver, but it's still tempting to seek out the best of the best.

The Rocky Mountains are beautiful viewed from below—from Denver for instance, as is the case with Inspiration Point Park (see p. 144).

The mountains also are stunning seen from above—from the air or from the summit of the highest mountains. Visitors can drive to the heights of 14,271-foot Mount Evans or 14,115-foot Pikes Peak to view what appear to be waves of mountains stretching on forever in all directions.

But for some, the best view of the mountains is on a level, from the mountains near Denver in Golden Gate Canyon State Park, a 12,000-acre state park a little under 30 miles from the Colorado State Capitol building.

The park's Panorama Point provides those miraculous views from about 9,300 feet above sea level, with vistas 100 miles up and down the Continental Divide, starting from 14,259-foot Longs Peak to the north.

Climbers can hike to Panorama Point via Mule Deer Trail. Drivers can drive there too.

Golden Gate Canyon State Park has a wide variety of visiting options, including campgrounds, cabins, yurts, and a four-bedroom/two-bathroom guest house.

Tremont Mountain dominates the center of Golden Gate Canyon State Park. A climb or drive to the heights of Panorama Point also offers views of the snowy peaks of the Continental Divide. Photo courtesy of Wikimedia Commons, Footwarrior

Coyote Trail is also recommended for its panoramas.

The park also offers a couple of fishing ponds, 12 hiking trails comprising 35 miles, serious climbing on Promontory Ridge, and wild animals that include black bears, bobcats, bighorn sheep, coyotes, moose, mountain lions, red foxes, and elk. Then there is its abundant bird life, including golden eagles and bald eagles.

Also, the park offers fishing for arctic grayling, brown trout, brook trout, cutthroat trout, and rainbow trout.

Golden Gate Canyon State Park also contains an amazing variety of plant life and a combination of grassland, aspen groves, sub-alpine forests, coniferous forest, wetlands, and ponderosa pine savanna. Finally, the park offers 125 picnicking sites. All for an $8 daily fee!

GOLDEN GATE CANYON STATE PARK

What: Golden Gate Canyon State Park isn't the largest or the highest, but there's lots that's special about it.

Where: 92 Crawford Gulch Rd., Golden

Cost: $8 daily; camping fees range from $18 to $36 for the Reverend's Ridge Campground. Reservations are required; just call 1-800-244-5613.

Pro Tip: Like almost all Colorado state parks, Golden Gate Canyon State Park allows dogs (on a six-foot or shorter leash).

WHEN FOUR DENVER REPORTERS HATCHED THE GREAT WALL OF CHINA HOAX

How did a sham that enthralled millions start in a Denver bar?

The year 1899 was big for Denver. National Jewish Health opened. Washington Park was designed and its development began. And the greatest hoax in the history of the Mile High City was hatched in a bar at the Oxford Hotel.

The Great Wall of China Hoax occurred because competition turned into conspiracy. The blazing hot newspaper war of the day brought together reporters from Denver's leading newspapers—the *Republican*, the *Times*, the *Rocky Mountain News*, and the only current survivor of the group, *The Denver Post*—to form a cabal to outwit their editors.

The four reporters had been ordered by their bosses to dig up something sensational. They ended up at Denver's Union Station, hoping to get a scoop. Not one came up with a thing.

Instead they decided to invent a Chicago engineer on his way to China to dismantle the Great Wall, break up its stones, and use them to build a road in its place.

Preposterous, you say? Yes, but in 1899, it would have taken weeks or months to check the story out.

Harry Lee Wilber, whose 1939 magazine article gave new life to the Great Wall of China Hoax, was a songwriter best known for "Back to Dear Old Denver Town."

GREAT WALL OF CHINA.
(Chicago Man Wants the Contract of Tearing It Down.)

The Great Wall of China Hoax began in a Denver bar and swiftly spread around the nation and the world. Years after one of its inventors debunked it, a new story revived and expanded the tall tale. Photo courtesy of Lima News, *1899*

The stories appeared on June 25, 1899. Oddly, none of them were published on their newspapers' front pages. The *Rocky Mountain News* never did run the story.

Yet newspapers around the country began picking up the tale, many adding fantastical embellishments.

Only one, *The New York Times*, ran stories doubting the yarn.

Forty years later, a Denver-based songwriter named Harry Lee Wilber wrote an article claiming that the hoax had triggered China's Boxer Rebellion, a war that claimed the lives of thousands. Wilber's article, a sham atop a scam, gave new life to the Great Wall of China Hoax. Years earlier, the last surviving reporter had confessed to the conspiracy.

ANATOMY OF AN INTERNATIONAL HOAX

What: Four Denver reporters, strapped for a story, invented a tall tale that became a global sensation.

Where: The only remaining newspaper of the four involved in the conspiracy is *The Denver Post*, 5990 Washington St.

Cost: Free

Pro Tip: All the locations pertinent to this saga remain in Denver, notably Union Station, 1701 Wynkoop St., and the Oxford Hotel, 1600 17th St.

COLORADO'S STRANGEST FESTIVAL IS AMONG THE MOST FUN

What is the weird tale behind Nederland's Frozen Dead Guy Days?

Colorado offers plenty of strange festivals, but for sheer oddity, none can match Nederland's Frozen Dead Guy Days.

Nederland is a mountain town of 1,445 souls situated 8,228 feet above sea level, about 17 miles west of Boulder.

It hosts a number of winter festivals, but there is only one Frozen Dead Guy Days, which does indeed celebrate a frozen dead guy. Or does it?

Here's the story: In 1989, a Norwegian named Trygve Bauge brought his deceased grandfather, Bredo Morstoel, to the United States in order to preserve his corpse in a California cryonics facility. In 1993, Trygve and his mother, Aud Morstoel, brought grandpa to Nederland, where they planned to create their own cryonics facility.

Mother and son kept granddad on ice, but then Trygve outstayed his visa and was deported. Aud, living in a home with neither electricity nor plumbing, was evicted. When it was discovered she was keeping a corpse on the property, she was ordered to remove it from Nederland or face fines and jail.

Amazingly, when her plight reached the media, Nederland relented and enacted a grandfather clause (no kidding)

The Tuff Shed where Bredo Morstoel's dead body is kept is also known as the International Cryonics Institute and Center for Life Extension, or ICICLE.

Within this Tuff Shed lies the body of Bredo Morstoel, cooled to 60 degrees below zero by being packed in 1,600 pounds of dry ice by Bo "Ice Man" Shaffer and a team of volunteers. Photo courtesy of Wikimedia Commons, Rick Pawl

exempting Aud's dad from the law prohibiting corpses on private property.

Responsibility for preserving Bredo's remains has since passed through a number of hands, raising concerns about how well the body has been preserved over the years.

The festival celebrates Bredo by offering a frozen winter swim, coffin obstacle races, frozen salmon tossing, and a dance called "Grandpa's Blue Ball," to name a few activities.

Also on offer are tours of the Tuff Shed where Bredo's remains are said to be kept. Tours of the shed's interior are included, although the body itself is not visible.

FROZEN DEAD GUY DAYS

What: A strange but enjoyable celebration of the reanimation aspirations of a visitor from Norway

Where: Go to Nederland. You can't miss it.

Cost: Outdoor event viewing is free; beer and food are available for a price; $25 for admittance to three live music tents.

Pro Tip: The three-day festival usually is held in mid-March, when Colorado weather is even less predictable than usual. Always remember: dress in layers.

REAL JURASSIC PARK

Why was Dinosaur Ridge declared a National Natural Landmark?

There are two sides to Dinosaur Ridge, one of the coolest places on Planet Earth. On one side is its significance. Dinosaur Ridge is important worldwide for its history, geology, and proximity to other incredibly cool locations.

On the other side, there is the fun factor. With a little imagination, visiting Dinosaur Ridge can feel like being caught in a dinosaur traffic jam.

Dinosaur Ridge is less than 15 miles west of downtown Denver. It's located in Morrison, just east of Red Rocks Park and Amphitheatre, and hard by Rooney Ranch, a pioneering homestead built in the 1860s.

The ridge played a central role in the history of paleontology. It was first excavated in 1877 by part-time Colorado School of Mines professor Arthur Lakes under the auspices of Othniel Charles Marsh. Marsh, the towering figure of 19th-century paleontology, was instrumental in the discovery of about 500 fossil species.

Among other species Lakes discovered at Dinosaur Ridge were the first specimens of Jurassic period *Allosaurus*, *Stegosaurus*, *Diplodocus*, and *Apatosaurus* dinosaurs.

Jurassic-era dinos are not the only species to have left traces behind at Dinosaur Ridge.

DINOSAUR RIDGE

What: One of the world's most significant dinosaur discovery centers

Where: 16831 West Alameda Pkwy., Morrison

Cost: Free, but it costs $11 for adults and $8 for children for full access to exhibit halls and a 45-minute guided bus tour.

Pro Tip: Be sure to walk Dinosaur Ridge Trail. It's just two miles long, but beware the sometimes scorching summers and frigid winters, and the 5,975-foot altitude.

Dinosaur Ridge hosts more than 200,000 visitors annually. Its Dinosaur Ridge Trail boasts more than 15 fossil and geologic sites and more than 300 sets of dinosaur tracks. Also worth a visit is nearby Morrison Natural History Museum, featuring the first Stegosaurus *and* Apatosaurus *fossils. Photo courtesy of Wikimedia Commons, footwarrior*

In 1937, workers digging West Alameda Parkway, which skirts both Dinosaur Ridge and Red Rocks Park, discovered Cretaceous-age dinosaur footprints. These were left behind by carnivorous dinosaurs and duck-billed herbivores—six new species of them—on the "Dinosaur Freeway," so-called because similar tracks have since been discovered all the way to northern New Mexico.

Dinosaur Ridge doubtless is far from having given up all its fossil secrets. But if you do discover a new specimen, it belongs to the government, not you. That's because in 1989, after decades of fossil pilfering in the area, the National Park Service declared the area a National Natural Landmark.

Dinosaur Ridge has been thoroughly adapted for visitors. Guided tours are available. It also has the Dinosaur Ridge Visitor Center, the Visitor Center Gift Shop, and the Dinosaur Ridge Discovery Center.

VIEWING THE COORS GEMS AND MINERALS HALL'S AMAZING COLLECTION

What famous artist once owned one of the world's biggest topaz gemstones?

The Denver gold rush began in 1857 and ended not long afterward. The Pikes Peak Gold Rush started in 1858—Pikes Peak or Bust!—drew about 100,000 hopefuls to Colorado, and petered out around 1861.

Even today, there are tourist attractions offering gold panning and gold mill and mine tours.

There's another way to enjoy Colorado's mining boom—the outstanding exhibits at the Denver Museum of Nature & Science.

The Coors Gems and Minerals Hall is easily overlooked. It's a bit tucked away at the end of a long hallway leading back from the museum entrance. To reach it, visitors venture down a long corridor mocked up as a mine entrance.

But once you reach the end of the entryway . . . wow.

The exhibit begins with a view into a Mexican silver mine, a cavern radiant with glittering gypsum crystals.

Diane's Pocket proves that Colorado's prospecting days are not behind it. The immense aquamarine was discovered in 2004 by Steve Brancato, then 33, a former high school dropout.

The Coors Gems and Minerals Hall features specimens such as the Alma King, left. Another excellent collection is to be found at the 15,000-square-foot Colorado School of Mines Geology Museum in Golden. See 2,500 items including the Miss Colorado Crown, with its 21 diamonds and 600 gemstones. Photo courtesy of Wikimedia Commons, Matt King

It follows with the Alma King, a six-foot-high wall featuring a stunning cherry-red rhombohedron-shaped rhodochrosite crystal from the Sweet Home Mine, a silver mine near Alma, Colorado.

Other highlights include Diane's Pocket, the largest pocket of aquamarine ever found in North America. Discovered on Mount Antero, Colorado's 10th highest mountain, the section measures 37 inches by 25 inches. It contains more than 100 aquamarine crystals, plus mica, garnets, black quartz crystals, and white feldspar.

THE COORS GEMS AND MINERALS HALL

What: The minerals exhibition at the Denver Museum of Nature & Science is bound to astonish.

Where: 2001 Colorado Blvd.

Cost: General museum admission: adults, $19.95 ($18.95 online); seniors, $16.95 ($15.95 online); youth (3–18), $14.95, ($13.95 online)

Pro Tip: The Denver Museum of Nature & Science has many outstanding exhibits. Some, such as its Prehistoric Journey dinosaur hall, are specific to Colorado and well worth your time.

The exhibit contains hundreds of mineral specimens from around the globe: Australian opals, California watermelon tourmaline, green malachite, blue azurite, four-inch zeolite needle sprays, and a huge Brazilian topaz once owned by Spanish surrealist artist Salvador Dali.

For gold bugs, the hall's highlight is Tom's Baby, the largest hunk of gold ever found in Colorado. (For more on Tom's Baby, see p. 30.)

THREE WAYS TO TAKE A STAGECOACH TOUR

Where can you relive Colorado's stagecoach era?

In between the wagon trains west and the 1870 arrival of railroads in Denver, the stagecoach reigned.

Stagecoach travel developed in the Denver area following the 1859 discovery of gold alongside Cherry Creek. Six stations were called "mile houses" for their proximity to the intersection of Broadway and Colfax Avenue in Denver. Two remain: Four Mile Historic Park in Denver and Seventeen Mile House in Centennial.

Then there's another stage stop, of quite a different sort, in the mountains west of Denver.

The highlight of Four Mile Historic Park is Four Mile House, the metro area's oldest house, but there's more to the 12-acre park.

Four Mile House was built in 1859 for weary travelers as the stage stop nearest central Denver along the Cherokee Trail. As time went by, it became a dance hall, inn, and tavern. Today the park combines an events center and museum with a summer camp and other activities for kids such as open-fire cooking, butter-making, and gold panning.

Seventeen Mile House Farm Park is less developed but well worth a visit. Built in the 1860s, today's 33-acre park features tours offered by the Cherry Creek Historical Society of the

---

Hollywood romanticized stagecoach travel—even producing a 1946 Red Ryder movie called *Stagecoach to Denver*—but stagecoaches actually were dusty, dirty, jarring, jolting, and often just plain terrifying.

Colorado's mile houses (17 Mile House, above) actually were located between three and five miles apart. About 150 stagecoach stations in all operated between Kansas and California. Stagecoaches followed the Cherokee Trail from Oklahoma and Kansas's Smoky Hill Trail, then to mountain mining camps or mail trails to points west. Photo courtesy of Wikipedia, Thomas Stockman

original house, plus a restored barn, silo, and milk shed.

The "sort of" stagecoach station restoration is the Stage Stop, a bar and restaurant, dance hall, and concert venue in Rollinsville, about 40 miles west of downtown Denver and 20 miles west of Boulder. Built in 1868, the Stage Stop served Butterfield Overland Mail Co. deliveries between St. Louis and San Francisco.

The Stage Stop is almost due south of Nederland, which makes it a popular stop-off during that town's Frozen Dead Guy Days festival (see p. 168).

STAGECOACH TO DENVER

What: Stagecoaches were an important part of Denver history.

Where: Four Mile Historic Park: 715 South Forest St., Denver; 17 Mile House Farm Park: 8181 South Parker Rd., Centennial; Stage Stop Tavern: 60 Main St., Rollinsville

Cost: Four Mile Historic Park general admission: adults, $5; seniors (65+) and military (w/ ID), $4; youth (7–17), $3; six and under, free. 17 Mile House Farm Park and Stage Stop Tavern: free.

Pro Tip: Check out 4th Sundays at Four Mile Historic Park, featuring a story time and activities for kids, Four Mile House tours (for the first 10 visitors), reenactors, and monthly themes.

THE RISE AND FALL OF THE COLORADO KKK

How does Denver's sordid Ku Klux Klan history continue to haunt it?

Once upon a terrible time, the Ku Klux Klan ruled Colorado and its capital. Sanity prevailed, and the KKK long ago was uprooted from the state and the city. Yet echoes of the Klan's dreadful influence continue to be heard here.

At its height, or depths, the Colorado Klan was its second biggest state chapter, after Indiana. At the peak of its power, Klan membership boasted both Colorado's governor, Clarence Morley, and Denver's mayor, Ben Stapleton, which almost brings us to the present day.

Stapleton served as Denver mayor twice, first from 1923 to 1931. In 1923, Stapleton was close friends with John Galen Locke, the Colorado Klan Grand Dragon. He lied his way into the mayoralty, claiming that he believed racial and religious prejudice were un-American. But once elected, Stapleton appointed Klan members to most important city positions, including police chief.

Sickened Denver voters sought to recall the new mayor, but Stapleton went public with his membership, rallied Klan support, and easily defeated his recall opponent.

Stapleton soon made another U-turn. Behind his KKK police chief's back, he conducted vice raids that exposed at

---

Denverites at first forgave Ben Stapleton's KKK flirtation, naming the Stapleton neighborhood after him. In 2020, however, the neighborhood name was changed to "Central Park."

Klan history can be divided into waves. The first wave crested after the Civil War, during the Reconstruction period. Colorado's KKK arrived with the second wave, which arose after World War I. Its influence peaked in about 1925 and faded quickly during the Great Depression. Photo courtesy of Wikimedia Commons

least a dozen crooked Klan cops. Locke was outraged, and kicked Stapleton out.

Both men survived the split, and Stapleton not only returned as Colorado state auditor in 1933 but as Denver mayor from 1935 to 1947. The KKK remained a Colorado power, however, until the Great Depression killed it off.

The Colorado Klan receded, but its waves continued to break over the state. In 1992, Martin Luther King Jr. Day marchers turned on taunting Klan protesters, igniting a riot.

Stapleton himself was honored, then erased. In 2020, residents of Denver's Stapleton neighborhood voted overwhelmingly to change the neighborhood's name to Central Park.

KKK GRAVE SITES

What: Denver was once virtually run by the KKK. Few traces of its malign influence remain.

Where: John Galen Locke's grave can be found in Denver's Fairmount Cemetery, 430 S. Quebec Street. Benjamin F. Stapleton was buried in Olinger Crown Hill Cemetery, 7777 W. 29th Ave., Wheat Ridge.

Cost: Fairmount Cemetery: $5 per location request. See the cemetery Welcome Center. Olinger Crown Hill Cemetery: ask for the grave location and a map at the cemetery administration building.

Pro Tip: For more on Colorado and the KKK, see: *Hooded Empire: The Ku Klux Klan in Colorado* by Robert Alan Goldberg, and Phil Goodstein's *In The Shadow of the Klan: When the KKK Ruled Denver 1920–1926*.

BEHOLD THE BEAUTY AND MYSTERY OF ROXBOROUGH STATE PARK

Which park near Denver is both a Red Rocks treasure and an archaeological district?

Roxborough State Park, about 300 million years and 25 miles southwest of the Colorado State Capitol, contains layer upon layer of history and geology.

The main impression the 3,339-acre park leaves is its staggering beauty and majesty. But it also has a hidden side, as the Roxborough State Park Archaeological District.

Roxborough's outstanding feature is its towering red rock formations, rising hundreds of feet at a dramatic 60-degree angle. Roxborough's red rocks are one of a number of similar formations up and down the Front Range of the Rocky Mountains, from Boulder to the north to Colorado Springs to the south. These include Boulder's Flatirons formation, Denver's Red Rocks Park and Amphitheatre, and Garden of the Gods and Red Rock Canyon, both in Colorado Springs.

Each of these is grand and glorious, and each is strikingly different from the others. All are the result of Fountain Formation outcrops. Most are strikingly red, due to their colored sandstone.

Roxborough Park scored a hat trick: designations as a State Natural Area in 1979, a National Natural Landmark in 1980, and a National Archaeological District in 1982.

ROXBOROUGH PARK

What: Douglas County's Roxborough State Park has something for every visitor.

Where: 4751 East Roxborough Dr., Littleton

Cost: $8 for a daily pass

Pro Tip: Bring your camera but leave Rover behind—Roxborough is the only state park that does not admit dogs.

The first description of Roxborough comes from 1820, when US Army Major Stephen Harriman Long explored the South Platte River area and saw, "a range of naked and almost perpendicular rocks rising abruptly to a height of 150 to 200 feet." Photo courtesy of Wikimedia Commons, Kristal Kraft

Roxborough offers five hiking trails that range from pretty easy to very easy, a couple in the shade of the enormous red rock upthrusts. A sixth hike, the six-mile-plus Carpenter Peak Trail, is significantly harder than the others.

Its outstanding hike is the two-mile-long Fountain Valley Trail, which takes the hiker/walker past most of the spectacular red rocks. At its base are the remains of one of the park's two historic homesteads, the handmade stone Persse Place. A spur off the main Fountain Valley Trail, the half-mile Fountain Valley Overlook, leads about 250 feet to a panoramic view of the valley.

As an archaeological district, Roxborough includes 12 sites containing evidence of habitation by Paleo-Indians and Native Americans from 5,000 BC to 1,000 AD. For more, ask at the Visitors Center.

BEARS, MOUNTAIN LIONS, AND MOOSE ON THE LOOSE

Why did Colorado's moose population explode?

The Denver metro area hosts more than three million people and an unknown number of foxes, coyotes, bears, bobcats, buffalo, deer, elk, mountain lions, and moose.

Most of these creatures stay in rural areas, or at least in the suburbs on the periphery of the city, but there are exceptions. Foxes, coyotes, and deer are liable to be seen almost anywhere in the metro region, including Denver proper. Bobcats and mountain lions, thankfully, are less frequent visitors.

Mountain lions avoid central Denver but have been spotted in Boulder and the Boulder area with some frequency. In 2018, for instance, a mountain lion broke into a house in Boulder a few blocks from the county courthouse, killed a house cat, and hung around for an hour before police and wildlife officers chased it out the front door.

Bear sightings are scarcely less rare, especially in Boulder, tucked up against the mountains as it is. In 2019, Boulder officials issued a Bear Warning due to the number of bears fresh out of hibernation roaming near the central city.

Not too many years ago, moose sightings in Colorado were exceedingly rare. Not any more. The moose population has

MUD LAKE

What: The best place to find moose in the greater metro area? Try Mud Lake near Nederland.

Where: Mud Lake, County Road 126, Nederland

Cost: Free

Pro Tip: Never approach a moose. Never feed one. Never cut off its escape route. Stay 100 yards away.

For an incredible near-urban viewing experience a half-hour from the Colorado State Capitol, see the Rocky Mountain Arsenal National Wildlife Refuge, 6550 Gateway Rd., Commerce City. Wildlife there includes bald eagles and more than 280 bird species, plus bison, coyotes, foxes, and two types of deer. See p. 2 for more information. Photo courtesy of Wikimedia Commons, Greg Talley

burgeoned in the Centennial State. According to the Colorado Parks and Wildlife department, the state's moose population jumped to 3,015 in 2016 from 1,270 in 2007.

In 2017, a moose was spotted by the Men's Wearhouse store in the Flatiron Crossing shopping complex in Broomfield, about 18 miles north of downtown Denver. Police surrounded the moose, tranquilized it, and moved it to South Park, about 100 miles away.

The thing is, moose can stand six feet high and weigh up to 1,200 pounds, and they are not afraid of humans. So be careful.

Colorado's moose population was near zero until, in 1978, the state began importing them from Wyoming and Utah to places far from Denver. They've migrated closer and closer ever since.

THE CANNIBAL WHOSE LEGEND WON'T DIE

Alferd Packer ate his companions. But did he murder them?

Colorado can't get enough of Alferd Packer, the state's favorite cannibal.

Born in Pennsylvania in 1842, Packer tried his luck as a soldier, ranch hand, wagon driver, hunter, farm worker, and miner, and failed at all of them.

In 1873, Packer talked his way into a group of men making their way from Utah to the newly discovered gold fields of Breckenridge, Colorado. He claimed to be a mountain guide. He lied.

By January, heavy winter snows had set in, and the men were becoming desperate. Luckily, they stumbled on a band of Ute Indians and their chief, Ouray, who was famously friendly to whites. Most of the travelers decided to stay with Chief Ouray until spring, but 11 decided to press on.

Six of the 11 chose a route Chief Ouray said would be safer; Packer persuaded five to travel through the mountains. What happened next has been disputed ever since.

What is known is that in April 1874, Packer staggered alone into the Los Pinós Indian Agency near Saguache, Colorado. He stayed in Saguache, spending money freely.

Long story short, a couple of Utes later entered Saguache with strips of dried human flesh. Packer collapsed, then

---

Packer was rescued from prison largely through the efforts of *The Denver Post* reporter Polly Pry. After his release he worked as a guard at the *Post.*

For a fun introduction to Packer, see the University of Colorado's Alferd Packer Restaurant & Grill, featuring Al's Greens Salad Bar and El Canibal Mexican Specialties, at the University Memorial Center, 1669 Euclid Ave., Boulder. Photo courtesy of Flickr, Mitch Hell

begged for mercy, then told a tale of starvation, murder, and cannibalism.

His story boiled down to whether he had murdered his companions or whether they had agreed among themselves to eat those who had died naturally—and Packer was merely the last one standing.

Packer was jailed in Saguache, escaped, was recaptured, and was tried twice for his crimes. He was sentenced to 40 years in prison, then the longest sentence in US history. He served 18 years, and upon his release became a vegetarian.

He died in 1907 and was buried in the Littleton Cemetery in Littleton, Colorado.

ALFERD PACKER'S GRAVE

What: The Colorado cannibal whose infamy refuses to die

Where: Littleton Cemetery: 6155 South Prince St., Littleton, 10 miles from downtown Denver

Cost: Free

Pro Tip: The world center for Alferd Packer research is the Denver Public Library's Western History and Genealogy Department, 10 W. 14th Ave. Pkwy., Denver.

THE GOVERNOR, LEGISLATORS, AND A WHOLE LOT OF GHOSTS

What is going on in the capitol building's mysterious tunnels?

The Colorado State Capitol building is a prodigious structure. Modeled after the US Capitol, it is set on a rise at the foot of Denver's Capitol Hill district, a mile above sea level. Its exterior is constructed of Colorado white granite and topped by a dome covered in Colorado gold leaf.

Its interior is fashioned of Colorado Rose Onyx and White Yule Marble, both quarried in the state; radiant stained glass windows; and a capacious rotunda rising 180 feet from the main entrance.

Unlike the US Capitol Building, the State Capitol combines legislative and executive functions, housing the Governor's Office, the Lieutenant Governor's Office, the Colorado General Assembly, and a variety of other public and private entities.

Also, the capitol building is rife with ghosts and spirits and sits atop mysterious—some say sinister—tunnels.

Officially, the capitol tunnels connect the building's parking lot and nearby state buildings. A bill passed in 2012 giving the legislature authority over the tunnels, ending a longtime dispute with the governor's office.

Construction on the Colorado capitol building began in 1886 and lasted until 1894. The gold dome was added in 1908 on the 50th anniversary of the Colorado Gold Rush.

The capitol's golden dome was restored between 2012 and 2014 at a cost of $17 million. About 65 ounces of gold leaf measuring .9999 pure was used to gild the dome. It was extracted from the same Cripple Creek & Victor Gold Mining Co. mine from which the original gold came. Photo courtesy of Pixabay

But according to some, in the not-so-distant past, a network of tunnels radiated from the capitol building to almost all of downtown Denver.

The tunnels serve as storage areas for items that don't belong elsewhere in the capitol. For instance, there are the severed heads of a pair of bandit brothers, said to float around the tunnels.

Capitol police and other workers there report mysterious voices calling out their names, and televisions turning off and on without human intervention. A woman in Victorian dress is said to roam the building, following employees as they go about their work. Ghostly galloping horses can be heard on the capitol's main floor. A politician's mistress is said to plague the capitol elevators—or maybe they just don't work very well.

COLORADO STATE CAPITOL

What: The impressive Colorado Capitol building, where there's more than meets the eye

Where: 200 East Colfax Ave.

Cost: Tours are free.

Pro Tip: The capitol tunnels are closed to the public; capitol tours are on offer Monday through Friday from 10 a.m. to 3 p.m.

THE WOMAN BEHIND THE MAN BEHIND COLORADO'S FIRST GOLD STRIKE

Lewis Ralston first discovered Colorado gold. Who rediscovered Lewis Ralston?

There are all sorts of rushes. There's the land rush, the head rush, the quarterback rush, and the fraternity rush. But there's nothing like a gold rush.

Colorado's modern history began with the 1858 gold rush to Cherry Creek, in what is now Denver's Confluence Park. Or maybe it began with the Pikes Peak gold rush, also in 1858. History-making as these events were, neither marked the Centennial State's first real gold strike.

It turns out gold was first discovered in Colorado in 1850 by Lewis Ralston in what today is the City of Arvada, about 10 miles from Denver.

Ralston was on his way to California to join the gold rush there when he chanced to wet his pan in a creek and came up with $5 worth of gold. The creek was to be named Ralston's Creek. (Arvada also has a Ralston Road, Ralston Estates, Ralston's Crossing, and so on.)

GOLD STRIKE PARK

What: Colorado's first documented gold find

Where: 5555 W. 56th Ave., Arvada

Cost: Free

Pro Tip: The park connects Ralston Creek Trail and Clear Creek Trail. It's a fine place for an easy hike and also continues to host lots of gold panning!

Gold Strike Park boasts a 400-foot-long curved pedestrian bridge featuring a 100-foot-tall mast held by suspended cables. The bridge connects two hiking trail systems and of course commemorates Colorado's first gold strike. Photo courtesy of Wikimedia Commons, Jeffrey Beall

Ralston continued to California, but returned to Colorado in 1858 and helped ignite the Cherry Creek gold rush.

Ralston's epochal first discovery was forgotten. Official recognition of his find went to William Greenberry Russell's prospecting at the confluence of Little Dry Creek and the South Platte River in 1858 in what is today Englewood.

Then Lois Lindstrom, a local historian and cofounder of the Arvada Historical Society, in the early 1990s proved that her city contained the site of the first gold discovery.

Lindstrom's research breakthrough occurred when she found an old aerial photograph of a cottonwood grove. It showed a place, long obscured by a trailer park, that was mentioned in a contemporaneous diary of Ralston's find.

Gaining official recognition of her discovery took more than 20 years. Later, the city recognized Ralston's strike and Lindstrom's rediscovery of it by creating Gold Strike Park, by Ralston Creek.

None of Colorado's earliest gold booms lasted long. Even the biggest early gold rush, the Pike's Peak Gold Rush, lasted only from July 1858 until about February 1861.

DENVER IS A GHOST TOWN, AND NOT IN A NICE WAY

Is Denver the spook capital of the United States?

The Denver area has a population of three million, and about a million ghosts.

We have already noted the spirits populating the Lumber Baron Inn & Gardens, the Brown Palace Hotel, the Oxford Hotel, Denver International Airport, and the Colorado State Capitol. But there's no way we can get to them all.

For instance, we noted some of the secrets of the University of Denver's Chamberlin Observatory, but not the spectral presence of Herbert Howe, the University of Denver's first professor of astronomy. Astronomy students often have observed Dr. Howe, who died in 1926, moving the observatory's telescope for them.

Historians actually might have pinpointed the origins of Denver's voluminous apparition population: the old Arapahoe County Courthouse.

Before 1902, Denver belonged to Arapahoe County. The basement of the old courthouse—since displaced by the Sheraton Denver Downtown Hotel—contained the Gates of Hell (see p. 12).

Almost any historic structure in Denver has its ghost stories: the Molly Brown House Museum, for instance, has phantom cigar smoke and a spooky rocking chair that rocks by itself.

The façade of Creswell Mansion, located at 1244 Grant St. in Denver's Capitol Hill neighborhood, features intricate carvings that include weird faces, dogs, and a sort of griffin. Inside, the building hosts ghostly presences that keep tenants' teeth on edge. Photo courtesy of flickr, Jeffrey Beall.

Whether the long-gone courthouse is the source of this phenomenon is debatable. But, in any case, Denver's ghost stories are virtually countless:

The old Dolly Madison ice cream store near South Colorado Boulevard and East Evans Avenue hosted a couple of long-deceased schoolgirls giggling at the soda fountain. Dolly Madison is long gone, but some say the girls' ghosts remain.

Charline Place, a sprawling apartment building built in 1890 not far from the Molly Brown House, has mysterious whispery voices to freak out its tenants.

We've already described Mattie Silks House of Mirrors. What we forgot to mention is that it is haunted: its doors sometimes rattle violently, its lights flash on and off, and its air turns cold and clammy without explanation. Of course today it is a disco, but that still doesn't explain it.

DENVER GHOST TOURS

What: Ghost stories are hard to avoid in Denver. So why try?

Where: Denver has numerous ghost tours. See darksideofdenver.com for some examples.

Cost: Most tours are in the $20-per-ticket range.

Pro Tip: Renowned Denver historians conduct ghost tours, notably Phil Goodstein and his Ghosts of Capitol Hill tours, and Kevin Pharris of Denver History Tours.

SOURCES

Urban Wilderness
Site visit; interview with Ryan Moehring, public information officer, US Fish & Wildlife Service; https://www.fws.gov/refuge/rocky_mountain_arsenal/; https://en.wikipedia.org/wiki/Rocky_Mountain_Arsenal_National_Wildlife_Refuge

The Strange Case of Buffalo Bill's Body
Site visit; interview with Bob Richard, guide, Grub Steak Expeditions; True West, Dec. 7, 2016, "Buffalo Bill Lies Here—Or Here"; *Los Angeles Times*, July 16, 2015, "Buffalo Bill's remains lie in Colorado. But Wyoming begs to differ."

A Literal Boomtown
Site visit; http://laruesviews.blogspot.com/1991/06/june-19-1991-louviers.html; Westword, March 11, 1999, "Blast From the Past"; https://coloradoencyclopedia.org/article/louviers; https://www.coloradohistoricnewspapers.org/cgi-bin/colorado?a=d&d=CTR19110720.2.57&e=-------en-20--1--img-txIN%7ctxCO%7ctxTA--------0--

Beyond the Big Top
Site visit; https://www.cpr.org/show-segment/whats-in-a-name-circus-showman-p-t-barnums-connection-to-denver/; https://303magazine.com/2013/10/concrete-canvas-denvers-spotlight-local-street-art/

A Dubious Culinary Landmark
Site visit; *Denver Post*, March 19, 2011, "Dorothy Ballast Jarrett, who ran the drive-in with the first cheeseburgers, dies at 94"; Westword, July 14, 2017, "Denver Food Inventions You Won't Find on the Official Slow Food Agenda"; https://www.thespruceeats.com/birth-of-the-cheeseburger-101426

The Gates of Hell at the Courthouse
Westword, Oct. 29, 2015, "Creep Show: Six Very Spooky Sites in Colorado"; http://historygoesbump.blogspot.com/2014/08/the-gates-of-hell-in-denver.html; https://www.cohauntedhouses.com/real-haunt/denver-courthouse.html

A Pen Big Enough for a Pachyderm
http://jvlbell.com/1859-denver-citys-elephant-corral/; https://unicoprop.com/properties/elephant-corral/; https://lodohistory.wordpress.com/lodo-destinations/the-elephant-corral/

A Dark Night in Hop Alley
Site visit; interview with Tom Noel; https://www.cpr.org/2019/09/02/on-halloween-nearly-150-years-ago-an-anti-chinese-riot-broke-out-in-denver/; https://www.historycolorado.org/story/colorado-voices/2019/04/11/rise-and-fall-denvers-chinatown

The Queen City's Blowtorch
https://www.auroragov.org/common/pages/DisplayFile.aspx%3FitemId%3D15760797&usg=AFQjCNGfdJxogENon-fwako2I52xcuRNzw; http://www.theradiohistorian.org/ge_stns/ge_stns.htm; https://www.radioworld.com/columns-and-views/a-fabulous-home-for-koa

Lost and Found Missile Silos
Site visit to Missile Park and perimeter of silo in Aurora; https://www.colorado.gov/pacific/cdphe/titan-1-missile-complexes; https://www.colorado.gov/pacific/cdphe/atlas-missile-sites; http://www.siloworld.net/SITES%20FOR%20SALE/SitesForSale.htm; https://big979.iheart.com/content/2019-04-25-you-can-now-own-a-creepy-colorado-missile-silo/; https://www.businessinsider.com/missile-silo-turned-castle-for-sale-in-kansas-2020-1; https://www.weldgov.com/departments/buildings_and_grounds/missile_site_park;

https://missilethreat.csis.org/missile/titan-i/; https://en.wikipedia.org/wiki/HGM-25A_Titan_I; https://www.mountainhome.af.mil/News/Article-Display/Article/1241029/peace-through-deterrence-the-titan-icbm-program/

Thirty Stories of Bricks
https://history.denverlibrary.org/news/worlds-tallest-smokestack-comes-tumbling-down; http://globevillestory.blogspot.com/2009/04/february-26-1950.html; http://buckfifty.org/tag/grant-smelter/; https://denverite.com/2018/12/10/vasquez-i-70-superfund-ou1-to-close-but-residents-fear-soil-pollution/

Asteroid Ranch
Site visit; *Denver Post*, Aug. 9, 2017, "In east Arapahoe County, West Bijou Ranch is home to one of the best places in the world to study Earth's fifth great extinction"; https://savory.global/west-bijou/; https://en.wikipedia.org/wiki/Cretaceous%E2%80%93Paleogene_boundary

Denver's Psychedelic Canine
Site visit; https://www.thetaleofthedog.com/; Westword, Aug. 16, 2017, "The Tale of the Dog Tells the Story of the Family Dog, the Rock Venue"; https://cmhof.org/inductees/exhibits/barry-fey/; https://concerts.fandom.com/wiki/Family_Dog_Denver

John Brisben Walker: A Castle and a Dream
Site visit; American Heritage, Oct. 1973, "The Summer White House In The Clouds"; https://www.jeffco.us/1332/Mount-Falcon-Park; https://coloradoencyclopedia.org/article/red-rocks-park-and-amphitheatre; https://morrisonhistory.org/people/john-brisben-walker/; https://kdvr.com/news/unique-2-colorado/colorados-castle-styled-summer-white-house/

The Golden Child
Interview with Dr. James Hagadorn, Tim & Kathryn Ryan Curator of Geology, Denver Museum of Nature & Science; Summit Daily, Dec. 7, 2015, "Discovering Tom's Baby, the largest piece of gold ever found in Colorado"; https://www.dmns.org/media/4715/annals-4-geology.pdf

Stone Forest in Rosedale
Site visit; https://en.wikipedia.org/wiki/Kunming; https://www.atlasobscura.com/places/shilin-stone-forest; https://www.denversistercities.org/kunming-china/; https://en.wikipedia.org/wiki/Flying_Tigers; *Denver Post*, April 13, 2019, "John Hua Yee of Flying Tiger fame, revered Aurora Chinese community elder, dies at 97"

Snoozing Slide
Site visit; https://www.dcla.net/bear-creek-park-playground; https://www.roadsideamerica.com/story/23598

Denver's False Start
Site visit; https://en.wikipedia.org/wiki/Montana_City,_Colorado; https://www.historycolorado.org/sites/default/files/media/documents/2018/mss.00023_auraria_town_company.pdf

A Thrilling Time Capsule
Site visit; interview with Brenda Fishman, manager, Lakeside Amusement Park; Westword, July 17, 2018, "Lakeside Amusement Park Has Survived 110 Years of Ups and Downs"; https://www.denverpost.com/2011/07/01/nostalgia-rides-on-at-lakeside/; https://history.denverlibrary.org/news/lakeside-amusement-park-celebrating-107-denver-summers; https://en.wikipedia.org/wiki/White_City_(Chicago); https://en.wikipedia.org/wiki/White_City_(amusement_parks)

First Amendment Landmark
Site visit; https://denverpressclub.org/; https://www.spj.org/news.asp?ref=736

Phantom Racetrack
Site visit; *Denver Post*, June 26, 2011, "The lure and lore of Lakeside track"; https://autoracingmemories.com/forums/showthread.php?t=15; https://thisusedtobedenver.tumblr.com/post/50909920028/this-used-to-be-lakeside-speedway

The Baron's Cow Palace
https://www.denvergov.org/content/denvergov/en/denver-parks-and-recreation/rentals-permits/rental-facilities/montclair-civic-center.html; Front Porch, Aug. 1, 2017, "Historic Montclair Home: Richthofen Castle"

Wash Park Dreaming
Site visit; https://en.wikipedia.org/wiki/Wynken,_Blynken,_and_Nod; https://www.youtube.com/watch?v=lsAR0Kc2zZs; https://dsmpublicartfoundation.org/artist/mabel-torrey/; https://www.historycolorado.org/location/eugene-field-house

Radioactive Streets
Site visit; Westword, June 26, 2003, "Room to Glow"; https://cumulis.epa.gov/supercpad/cursites/csitinfo.cfm?id=0800247; http://montrosecounty.granicus.com/MetaViewer.php?view_id=2&clip_id=141&meta_id=10184; https://www.denverpost.com/2009/11/22/cleanup-fund-for-radioactive-shattuck-chemical-site-quadruples-to-1-million/

Flood of the Century
Site visits; https://www.littletongov.org/my-littleton/littleton-history/other-topics/1965-flood-of-south-platte; https://www.confluence-denver.com/features/south_platte_river_vision_091014.aspx; https://www.cpr.org/show-segment/50-years-ago-devastating-flood-helped-shape-denver/

Five Points' House of Jazz
https://coloradoencyclopedia.org/article/rossonian-hotel; https://history.denverlibrary.org/rossonian-hotel; https://denverarchitecture.org/site/rossonian-hotel/

A Little Saigon in Denver
Site visit; interview with Father Joseph Dang, priest and chaplain; https://www.youtube.com/watch?v=d6QL5BxRt9w; *Denver Post*, Feb. 18, 2014, "Little Saigon Business District designated as Vietnamese cultural area in west Denver"; https://kdvr.com/news/local/denvers-little-saigon-to-achieve-beautification-amid-safety-projects/

The Spider Man of Denver
Interview with Rich Grant, consultant, Visit Denver; https://en.wikipedia.org/wiki/Theodore_Edward_Coneys; https://web.archive.org/web/20040213070643/http://www.prisonmuseum.org/spider.htm

A Baseball Diamond
Site visit; interview with Joey Schor, marketing/promotions director, National Ballpark Museum; https://ballparkmuseum.com/

Foothills Fortress
https://cherokeeranch.org/; https://coloradoencyclopedia.org/article/cherokee-ranch-and-castle

Denizens of the Diorama
https://denverite.com/2018/01/07/elves-hidden-throughout-denver-museum-nature-science-went-looking/; https://www.dmns.org/media/2185/elf-scavenger-hunt-2017-english.pdf; https://www.atlasobscura.com/places/hidden-elves-at-the-denver-museum-of-nature-and-science; https://www.cpr.org/show-segment/

its-one-of-denvers-cutest-secrets-hidden-elves-in-the-nature-and-science-museum/; https://www.9news.com/article/life/hidden-elves-hanging-out-at-the-museum-of-nature-and-science/73-559719466

Rocky Mountain Mardi Gras
https://www.historycolorado.org/sites/default/files/media/document/2018/ColoradoMagazine_v25n4_July1948.pdf; https://www.atasteofcolorado.com/home/about/; https://history.denverlibrary.org/news/festival-mountain-and-plain-1895; *Colorado Daily Chieftain*, September 27, 1898, "FESTIVAL OF MOUNTAIN AND PLAIN, DENVER, OCTOBER 4, 5 AND 6"; https://coloradoartifactual.com/colorados-slaves-of-the-silver-serpent-18/

We All Scream for Ice Cores!
https://icecores.org/; http://waisdivide.unh.edu/

Eggs Mark the Spot
Site visit; https://samsno3.com/2018/10/31/exploring-the-mystery-behind-a-breakfast-classic-the-denver-omelette/; https://www.atlasobscura.com/places/denver-omelet-plaque

A Sundial Rises from the Rubble
http://denverhilltop.com/neighborhood/parks/cranmer-park/; https://www.atlasobscura.com/places/cranmer-park-sundial; http://coloradopreservation.org/sundial-plazacranmer-park/

Before Buses: Denver's Lost Trolleys
https://denverurbanism.com/2017/08/the-history-of-denvers-streetcars-and-their-routes.html; https://en.wikipedia.org/wiki/Denver_Tramway; https://coloradopreservation.org/2015-list-colorados-most-endangered-places/denver-tramway-company-streetcar-no-4; http://www.denvertrolley.org/

Red Rocks: Behind the Scenes
https://coloradoencyclopedia.org/article/red-rocks-park-and-amphitheatre; https://redrockshistory.org/history/1928-1941/building-the-amphitheatre/; https://theknow.denverpost.com/2013/05/02/barry-fey-cannot-be-buried-in-morrison-cemetery-near-red-rocks-amphitheatre/68036/; Westword, June 11, 2012, "Red Rocks' famous hidden tunnel: A peek at the rock star signatures beneath the stage"; https://www.concertarchives.org/venues/red-rocks-amphitheatre--11; https://en.wikipedia.org/wiki/Red_Rocks_Amphitheatre; *Denver Post*, June 2, 2016, "75 facts about Red Rocks"; The Gazette, April 15, 2019, "The secret tunnel at Red Rocks Amphitheatre where stars leave their mark"

Dam No More
https://cpw.state.co.us/placestogo/parks/CastlewoodCanyon; https://coloradoencyclopedia.org/article/castlewood-dam; https://damfailures.org/case-study/castlewood-canyon-dam-colorado-1933/; https://www.historycolorado.org/grant-news/preservation/2002/05/01/where-were-you-when-dam-broke-castlewood-canyon-booklet-collects

I. M. Pei's Living City
Westword, May 18, 2019, "IM Pei Is Gone, and So Are Two of His Denver Architectural Wonders"; https://en.wikipedia.org/wiki/I._M._Pei; *Denver Post* / Bloomberg, May 16, 2019, "IM Pei, architect of Denver's 16th Street Mall, dies at 102"; https://en.wikipedia.org/wiki/List_of_I._M._Pei_projects; Conversations with IM Pei: Light is the Key by Gero Von Boehm

An Igloo, Rattlesnakes, and FDR
https://www.historycolorado.org/historic-resources-camp-george-west; https://historicjeffco.files.wordpress.com/2012/01/hj2011grunska.pdf; https://livingnewdeal.org/projects/colorado-amphitheater-golden-co/; https://en.wikipedia.org/wiki/Colorado_Amphitheater

Denver's Vanishing Messiah
ellisnelson.com/2012/11/29/the-curious-case-of-francis-schlatter-the-denver-messiah/

Lamb Spring's Prehistoric Secrets
Site visit; lambspring.org; en.wikipedia.org/wiki/Lamb_Spring

The Baffling Disappearance of Prof. Thomas Riha
academeblog.org/2016/10/06/the-disappearance-of-thomas-riha-an-unsolved-academic-mystery/; colorado.edu/coloradan/2019/03/01/thomas-riha-mystery

Colorado's Second-Greatest Diamond Swindle
law.justia.com/cases/colorado/supreme-court/1971/24116.html; en.wikipedia.org/wiki/Great_Diamond_Hoax

Colorado Chautauqua Brings Back the Good Ol' Days
Site visit; chautauqua.com; bouldercolorado.gov/parks-rec/chautauqua-park

Denver's Cold War Time Machine
Site visit; fema.gov/fema-regions/colorado; barthworks.com/lakewoodcohistory/historiclocations/bldg710/bldg710.htm

Historic Elitch Theatre to Rise Again . . . and Again
Site visit; historicelitchtheatre.org; etfest.com

A Pristine Trip Back to Gold Boom Times
en.wikipedia.org/wiki/Eldora_Historic_District; historycolorado.org/location/eldora-historic-district

Denver's Shocking Cold Case
blogs.denverpost.com/coldcases/2013/06/08/fathers-day-massacre-at-united-bank/6917/4/; huffpost.com/entry/denver-fathers-day-massacre-james-king_n_3423381

Shhh . . . Spooky Secrets of Denver's Lumber Baron Inn
Site visit; lumberbaron.com; www.legendsofamerica.com/co-lumberbaron

The 5 Star Salt Caves Secret
Site visit; 5starsaltcaves.com; tripadvisor.com/Attraction_Review-g33388-d11832950-Reviews-5_Star_Salt_Caves-Denver_Colorado.html

Riddles of Denver International Airport
Site visit; flydenver.com; en.wikipedia.org/wiki/Denver_International_Airport

Linger Eatuary's Deathly Secrets
lingerdenver.com; atlasobscura.com/places/linger-eatuary

The Mystery of the Denver Mint Stickup
Site visit; usmint.gov/about/mint-tours-facilities/denver/visiting-the-denver-mint; doingdenver.com/denver-mint-tours.html

Mother Cabrini, Colorado Miracle Worker
mothercabrinishrine.org; mothercabrini.org/what-we-do/spiritual-ministries/mother-cabrini-shrine-golden-colorado/

Mattie Silks, Her House of Mirrors, and the Naked Duel
Site visit; en.wikipedia.org/wiki/Mattie_Silks; Braun, Matthew. Mattie Silks. Pinnacle Books, 1985.

Denver Players/Denver Sugar's Seedy Saga
www.westword.com/news/brenda-stewart-denver-players-sugar-owner-and-ex-escort-indicted-for-tax-evasion-racketeering-5910210; glendalecherrycreek.com/2018/03/hancocks-sex-scandals-erupt/

How a "Miraculous" Deal Saved a Half-Hidden Gem
holyghostchurch.info; facebook.com/holyghostchurch

Ghostly Guests at the Lavish Brown Palace Hotel
Site visit; www.brownpalace.com; en.wikipedia.org/wiki/Brown_Palace_Hotel_(Denver,_Colorado)

An Architectural and Astronomical Marvel
Site visit; www.denverastro.org/?page_id=64; chamberlainobservatory.com

Denver's All-Time Con King
www.soapysmith.net; www.historynet.com/soapy-smith-con-mans-empire.htm

Hidden Beauties
www.denvergov.org/content/denvergov/en/denver-parks-and-recreation/parks/mountain-parks.html

200 Miles of Sweeping Views
www.onlyinyourstate.com/colorado/denver/hidden-park-denver; www.denvergov.org/content/dam/denvergov/Portals/747/documents/planning/inspiration-point/InspirationPointPark_2019-Discovery-Outreach-ConceptDesign.pdf

The Gruesome Tale of Three Prominent Denver Parks
Site visit; en.wikipedia.org/wiki/Cheesman_Park,_Denver; botanicgardens.org/; tripadvisor.com/Attraction_Review-g33388-d560033-Reviews-Cheesman_Park-Denver_Colorado.html

Denver, the Mile High City, Measures Up
Site visit; quirkytravelguy.com/quirky-attraction-one-mile-above-sea-level-sign-at-the-colorado-state-capitol; www.dailymail.co.uk/sciencetech/article-2994105/At-theory-Denver-mile-sea-level.html

Where to Find the World's Best Clock
time.gov; www.nist.gov/pml/time-and-frequency-division/primary-standard-nist-f1

Shhh . . . Here's a Guide to Denver's Secret Bars
www.uncovercolorado.com/best-denver-speakeasies; www.thrillist.com/drink/denver/best-speakeasies-in-denver

Denver's Oldest Hotel . . . and Its Art Deco Bar
Site visit; www.theoxfordhotel.com/eat-drink/the-cruise-room; www.thrillist.com/venue/drink/denver/bar/the-cruise-room

A Self-Secret Way to See Denver's Union Station
Site visit; unionstationindenver.com; www.tripadvisor.com/Attraction_Review-g33388-d130318-Reviews-Denver_Union_Station-Denver_Colorado.html

The Money Museum and Its Free Bags Of Bills
www.tripadvisor.com/Attraction_Review-g33388-d2140615-Reviews-The_Money_Museum_at_the_Federal_Reserve_Bank_Denver_Branch-Denver_Colorado.html; fun-denver-attractions.com/denver-sightseeing-attractions-top/money-museum-denver-federal-reserve-bank/

In with the Old, In with the New
Site visit; www.marriott.com/hotels/travel/dendr-renaissance-denver-downtown-city-center-hotel; www.denverpost.com/2014/05/13/for-old-colorado-national-bank-building-a-renaissance

The Boulder Dushanbe Teahouse's Long, Strange, Magnificent Trip
Site visit; www.boulderteahouse.com; en.wikipedia.org/wiki/Dushanbe_Tea_House

Reach-Out-and-Touch-It View
Site visit; cpw.state.co.us/placestogo/Parks/goldengateCanyon; alltrails.com/parks/us/colorado/golden-gate-canyon-state-park

When Four Denver Reporters Hatched the Great Wall of China Hoax
www.thevintagenews.com/2017/02/25/four-denver-newsmen-started-the-1899-hoax-declaring-that-the-great-wall-of-china-was-to-be-dismantled/

Colorado's Strangest Festival Is Among the Most Fun
frozendeadguydays.org; en.wikipedia.org/wiki/Frozen_Dead_Guy_Days

Real Jurassic Park
Site visit; dinoridge.org; tripadvisor.com/Attraction_Review-g33561-d147095-Reviews-Dinosaur_Ridge-Morrison_Colorado.html

Viewing the Coors Gems and Minerals Hall's Amazing Collection
Site visit; dmns.org/visit/exhibitions/gems-and-minerals/; www.5280.com/2017/06/hidden-colorado-2/

Three Ways to Take a Stagecoach Tour
Site visit; www.fourmilepark.org; arapahoegov.com/Facilities/Facility/Details/17-Mile-House-Farm-Park-23; en.wikipedia.org/wiki/Seventeen_Mile_House

The Rise and Fall of the Colorado KKK
coloradoencyclopedia.org/article/ku-klux-klan-colorado; www.denverpost.com/2006/03/09/denvers-20s-roared-with-kkk-knavery

Behold the Beauty and Mystery of Roxborough State Park
Site visit; coloradoencyclopedia.org/article/roxborough-state-park-archaeological-district; cpw.state.co.us/placestogo/Parks/roxborough

Bears, Mountain Lions, and Moose on the Loose
urbanwildliferescue.org; bouldercolorado.gov/wildlife/urban-wildlife-issues

The Cannibal Whose Legend Won't Die
en.wikipedia.org/wiki/Alferd_Packer; lakecity.com/mountain-town-activities/historic-attractions/17-things-to-do/history/11-alferd-packer

Governor, Legislators, and a Whole Lot of Ghosts
Site visit; www.colorado.gov/capitol; en.wikipedia.org/wiki/Colorado_State_Capitol

The Woman Behind the Man Behind Colorado's First Gold Strike
arvada.org/city-hall/our-community/colorado-s-first-documented-gold-strike; findinggoldincolorado.com/hints-for-prospecting-goldstrike-park

Denver Is a Ghost Town, and Not In a Nice Way
legendsofamerica.com/co-denverghosts; theknow.denverpost.com/2017/10/03/denver-real-haunted-houses-ghosts-2017/159937; Schlosser, S. E., and Paul G. Hoffman. "*Spooky Colorado: Tales of Hauntings, Strange Happenings, and Other Local Lore*."

INDEX